Ryan's Master

Ryan's Master

The Story of John Whitaker

Jane Fuller

Foreword by John Whitaker

Stanley Paul
London Melbourne Sydney Auckland Johannesburg

Stanley Paul & Co. Ltd
An imprint of the Hutchinson Publishing Group
17–21 Conway Street, London W1P 6JD

Hutchinson Publishing Group (Australia) Pty Ltd
16–22 Church Street, Hawthorn, Melbourne, Victoria 3122

Hutchinson Group (NZ) Ltd
32–34 View Road, PO Box 40–086, Glenfield, Auckland 10

Hutchinson Group (SA) Pty Ltd
PO Box 337, Bergvlei 2012, South Africa

First published 1985
© Jane Fuller 1985

Phototypeset in Linotron Century
by Input Typesetting Ltd, London

Printed and bound in Great Britain by Anchor Brendon Ltd,
Tiptree, Essex

British Library Cataloguing in Publication Data

Fuller, Jane
Ryan's master: the story of John Whitaker.
1. Whitaker, John   2. Show jumpers (Persons)
—Great Britain—Biography
I. Title
798.2'5'0924   SF295.5

ISBN 0 09 162360 X

Contents

Acknowledgements

This book would have been impossible without the help of John and Clare Whitaker who gave so much time and thought to it, fitting numerous interviews into their already crammed schedule. I can't thank them enough.

Thanks also go to Donald and Enid Whitaker, Malcolm and Elaine Barr, Fred and Mavis Brown, Eleanor Fuller, Hazel Lord and to the many others who contributed.

I am grateful, too, to the following for allowing their photographs to be used in the book: Cindy Bowring, Clive Hiles, Kit Houghton, *Huddersfield Examiner*, Ian Kenvyn, Leslie Lane, Bob Langrish and the *Yorkshire Post*.

Foreword by John Whitaker

Show jumping was something I watched on television and read about in books until seeing people like David Broome and Harvey Smith encouraged me to have a go, but I never thought I could compete against them, let alone beat them – sometimes. However, I did *dream* that one day it would happen and, as I improved, that dream became my ambition.

Doing this book has brought back many happy memories. I started competing, as most children do, by hacking to local gymkhanas, going to Pony Club rallies and camps and then progressing to shows affiliated to the British Show Jumping Association. The highlights of my junior jumping days were qualifying for the Junior Foxhunter final at Hickstead and for the Leading Junior Show Jumper of the Year competition at Wembley.

I remember travelling to the shows in the early days when my mother drove the horsebox and put up the practice jumps for both me and my brother, Michael, and kept us on the 'straight and narrow', or tried to!

When Ryan's Son came to me I did not realize, at first, what a change he would make to my life. He was a bit odd-looking, but whatever I asked of him he did. He quickly went up through the grades and was soon helping me compete against – and beat – the likes of Harvey Smith and David Broome.

I have known Jane Fuller, the author of this book, from junior show jumping days and I worked on the book with her during the 1983 and 1984 seasons. These were particularly successful ones for me with silver medals coming at the European Championships and the Olympics, which I will never forget. I was enormously delighted to win the 1983 Jumping Derby at Hickstead. Ryan had jumped so well in it in previous years and had been unlucky not to win. I had always wanted to win that one. It's good to have a souvenir of such happy days.

We spend ten months of the year travelling from one show to the next, sometimes popping home for a few days in between. Most of the riders get on really well together and are ready to help each other with problems. It can be tiring but every time you win a competition it makes it all worthwhile and keeps you going.

So this is the story of my life and our aim also is to give you an insight into the life of an international show jumper – a look behind the scenes at what goes on at shows and in a show jumping yard. I hope you will find in it plenty to entertain as well as information about the sport.

Jane Fuller and I agreed that it should be written in language that everyone can understand, partly because we know that many show jumping fans do not have a detailed knowledge of riding and partly because the people in the sport are informal and down-to-earth. I believe that you can be too technical and my philosophy is: 'Get on and do it'.

I hope you will enjoy the book and that it will help you to understand the sport – especially if you are young. If your interest in show jumping is intensified and made to last longer by what you read, then I shall be happy.

1

First Steps

It's not often you see Yorkshiremen weep, but plenty of them did as John Whitaker clinched the silver medal for Britain in the team show jumping event at the 1984 Olympic Games.

When John went into the ring he knew Ryan's Son could knock down one fence and still help Britain to win the silver. But the sixteen-year-old horse had had four fences down in the first round and nail-biting fans feared it would be impossible for John to conjure the necessary improvement.

When he made an error at fence eight, a spread over water, only the brave could bear to watch as he approached the most difficult section of the course. John has often been described as unflappable, but now we'll have to invent a new word: even he had never faced pressure like that before, yet he came up trumps, sailing over the rest of the course with only ¾ of a time fault to add to his 4 faults.

Afterwards John said, 'I just walked him round between the two rounds and then jumped a few small fences. He touched one and that did him good. He was so full of himself I had difficulty getting him to concentrate.' John steered clear of the main collecting ring, where Ryan did not like the going, and removed his spurs.

He realized time faults would put Britain out of a medal place if he had two fences down. 'I didn't worry about that, I was going for the silver,' he said.

His brother, Michael, had set the team up for a storming finish with a clear on Overton Amanda early in the second round. He said it was more nerve-racking watching John than jumping his own rounds.

The proudest person in the 32,000 crowd was John and Michael's father, Donald. Fighting back the tears, he said, 'I wanted to go away while they were jumping, but I just couldn't move. I'm glad I stuck it now. When I saw all the pressure on John's shoulders, I thought, "That's the man to have there." I knew he would get things together.' Mr Whitaker had always said Ryan would be right for the Olympics, when others were concerned about putting the horse through such a test at his age.

Watching the competition at home on television, at the Pennine farm where John and Michael grew up, was their mother, Enid, who taught the boys to ride. John's wife, Clare, and their two children, Louise, aged four, and Robert, one, had also been rooting for him long distance.

* * * *

Edwin John was born on 5 August 1955, the first of Enid and Donald Whitaker's four sons. The family's 100-acre cattle, sheep and pig farm lies below the M62 between Halifax and Huddersfield. Its steep pastures, criss-crossed with stone walls, stretch away from urban West Yorkshire towards the Pennines. Two haphazard rows of farm buildings were once converted to thirty stables and stalls, largely by John's handiwork. The only flat paddock in sight, little bigger than a suburban garden, was the boys' training ground.

John's parents were from farming families with a tradition of working with horses; both of them rode as youngsters. Mrs Whitaker had competed at a few local shows and John's father had always driven horses. Their families could not afford to keep competition horses or take the children to shows every week. In fact, Mr Whitaker's father had a dour Yorkshire suspicion of the circus-style show scene: he thought that horses should earn their keep.

It was Mrs Whitaker who taught the boys to ride and John has never had another coach. Her practical philosophy was that you learn from experience, making progress through solving problems and by watching the successes and failures of others. She also had a sound knowledge of the correct way to ride and, with gentle reminders such as, 'Keep your heels down,' she stopped them developing bad habits. However, she did not try to drum a rigid riding position into the boys at the expense of comfort and confidence. John always stuck his elbows out a bit, but as this did not affect his control his mother let it go.

John may have had horses in his blood, but he had to develop his raw talent the hard way, through years of trial and error with a multitude of rides. There were always horses on the farm. John can remember the old carthorses grazing away their retirement while the tractors that had replaced them worked the fields. Ponies were still used for pulling the Whitaker milk float and it was an old mare, who had spent most of her life between the traces, who became John's first pony. Peggy was a good-looking black mare, about 13 hands high. Mr Whitaker believes she would not have looked out of place in a show ring, but circumstances dictated that she earn her keep. John's father at first adhered to his own father's view: horses were for work, not for dashing around the show circuit.

Before he was old enough to go to school John mastered the art of staying aboard Peggy, but she was soon ready for retirement and needed replacing. Mr Whitaker bought a pony in the village; however, he was hardly the bombproof little gentleman on which a child from a more wealthy family would have learned. Silver's problems started even before he left the yard. He napped, which meant he was loath to leave his pals in the stable. His method of evasion was to go backwards, stubbornly disobeying every command from the rider. John remembers his dapper father having to get on the pony to straighten him out, before he could take over. But this was only a temporary measure and gradually he mastered Silver.

The pony not only became obedient to the basic signals John used while hacking about farmland and lanes, he also improved and John began to ask more of him. They learned together because no one in the family had ever taught a horse any of the 'tricks' needed for competition. One of the experiments John tried with Silver was jumping. The first obstacle tackled by the future champion comprised two bricks and a slat of wood. The lessons went well and John built up the challenge to four bricks at each end of the pole. Once Silver could jump that – about 18 inches – easily, he began to think about entering his first show. He set his sights on Huddersfield's annual event in Greenhead Park and arrived confident he could win. But the fences had coloured poles and various types of filling, which the pony had never seen before. John was unabashed and set sail for the first fence, which had a brush under the pole. The pony refused to go near it and after three attempts the pair were eliminated.

This setback acted as a goad to John; he was determined not to be beaten. He set his sights on getting round a show jumping course and at home he built a variety of fences, including a brush, to train the pony to cope with all the surprises show organizers could spring. At each subsequent show Silver got further round until eventually he completed a course, albeit with faults. John's mother helped with this early training, pointing out where his riding errors had let the pony defy him. But father was still suspicious. To him a competition pony was just hanging around costing money.

However, when it became clear that horses were providing John – and his brothers – with chances to succeed, as well as to enjoy themselves, Mr Whitaker soon came round and became an ardent supporter. It was typical of John's childhood that he was not indulged, but once it emerged that he was heading in a fruitful direction the whole weight of family pride and loyalty swung behind him. His childhood was above all secure. Living on a farm provided the children with plenty to do, whether it was chores or opportunities to play. John was never short of company. His brothers, Steven and Michael, two and five years his junior, shared his interest in ponies. Ian, the baby of the family, born six years after John, also learned to ride as a toddler. John's mother was their mentor and soon set

4

up a riding school to make some extra money to supplement the sport.

The family's values were traditional and straightforward; few questions were raised about what was right and wrong. Hard work and reliability were high on the lists of virtues, and anything that smacked of a disregard for parental expectation received short shrift. All the boys went to Sunday school – until shows took over the Sabbath. John pursued his growing interest in riding with all the support his parents could muster. After the early adjustment in attitude, his parents found show jumping was a sport that involved the whole family, cementing bonds and fitting in naturally with farming. John, an easy going, placid person, had established his aims without rocking the boat.

His mother was the stricter parent, always insisting that things were done properly. One of John's ponies had four white socks and he always feared that the pre-show inspection by Mum would reveal some offending stain. His father put on a stern face – no Yorkshireman likes to appear soft – but was actually the easier one to get round.

At school John and his brothers got on well with the other children, although their passion for ponies kept them apart at evenings and weekends. John did not take lessons seriously, always confident that he was heading for a farming career. He enjoyed all sport, representing his school at rugby and cross-country running.

He was always fit and healthy and had a horror of being confined to bed through illness or injury. His only spell in hospital came when he broke his foot bringing a horse in from a field. He had just closed the gate behind the animal and jumped on it for a bareback ride up a steep lane to the yard. No sooner was he on top than the horse fell and rolled on John's foot, crushing it against the cobble stones. He was in hospital for three weeks, regretting every moment of lost riding. It made him even more determined to make progress when he came out. A couple of years later he split his head open trying to vault on to a cantering pony, a move known as the 'Indian jump'. He was wearing baggy trousers and the pony trod on the flared bottoms. John fell flat on his back and the pony kicked his head. There was plenty of blood and his worried parents took him to hospital. But John was adamant he did not want a repeat stay and on the way, when the car paused, he leapt out and started running. It took a while for his parents to recapture him and drag him to casualty, where a few stitches were all that was needed.

John's general knowledge of horses benefited from the riding school his mother ran. He would help with feeding, mucking out and grooming and, in his teens, would sometimes take out rides. His mother did all the instructing and he never dreamed of doing any teaching himself. He was an instinctive rider and would have found it difficult to explain how and why he did things – even if he had had the confidence to try.

The riding school became so popular that some of the show jumping ponies were roped in to carry the pupils, and occasionally John's mother would lead out the hacks on a bicycle. A girl was employed as a groom but on her days off John had to step in. He missed some school because he was needed to help at home and other days fell by the wayside when he went to mid-week shows. He was never heading for O-levels at Salendine Nook secondary modern school and so attendance was not regarded as a priority, a view with which the school inspectors disagreed. However, in his last couple of years he did see the need to improve his performance at the basic subjects, and the extra effort brought better marks; but his motivation remained limited because of his conviction that a career in farming lay before him.

*   *   *   *

John was given his first good pony at the age of about eight. Bonnie, only 11 h.h. and strong and fiery, cost £20. He was still partly a stallion, which aggravated his hot temperament. Castration had failed to remove both testicles, one having remained inside his body. A horse like this, called a rig, shows aggressive, stallion-like behaviour, as well as retaining the ability to sire foals. The Whitakers were able to get Bonnie properly gelded and John set to work to master the little devil. In the process he learned a quiet, patient style of riding which set the pattern of his horsemanship.

Bonnie did not need any urging to tackle show jumps. Once John had calmed his excitable temperament and found, with the held of a curb bit, the key to controlling him, he became a winner. Prizes rolled in both for gymkhana events and show jumping. Bonnie was so brave that he would tackle courses for 13.2 h.h. ponies, thus competing against animals more than 8 inches bigger than himself. His successes were such that within two years of acquiring the pony, John's father was offered £200 for him. Mr Whitaker needed the money, but by that time he knew how much horses meant to his son and would not have dreamt of selling such a good animal. It was a source of pride to John and the family that the pony's value had increased tenfold in his hands. And John revelled in beating, on his home-spun bargain, ponies which cost £200 or £300.

But Bonnie was also to teach him that disaster can strike at any time in show jumping. At a show in Cheshire John had jumped a clear with Bonnie and his jump-off round was going well when the pony seemed to paddle in mid-air over a fence. He came down on his nose, twisted over and lay still. John was winded and for a moment the two lay side by side, motionless. John's parents waited for them to get up and soon John struggled to his feet. But the pony did not. Urgent appeals for a vet went out over the public address system. When he arrived at Bonnie's side he said the pony had died of a broken neck. John, who was only twelve, and had enjoyed a near unbeatable run on the pony, was devastated. There were plenty of tears, but his wish to show jump was undiminished. He knew no blame could be attached to him for the pony's death. It was just a stroke of bad luck.

Later in life he put a positive interpretation on the tragedy. He believes it set in motion a train of events which led ultimately to Ryan's Son. Watching the accident was a

Mr Gregory, from Meltham, near Huddersfield. He felt sorry for John and bought him a 13.2 h.h. pony called Mustapha to ride. Mr Gregory was happy with John's successes with the pony and when the boy was fourteen bought him the next size up, a 14.2 h.h. skewbald called Crazy Horse. It was on that pony, which was no easy ride, that John caught the attention of Mr Malcolm Barr – who was to become the owner of Ryan's Son and John's father-in-law.

Soon after Bonnie died Ryan's Son was born in Ireland. He was the gawky offspring of a carthorse mare and a Thoroughbred stallion. While Ryan was gaining early strength guzzling the lush grass of County Wexford at Ned Byrne's farm, John still had plenty to learn about riding ponies.

2

Young Promise

In his teens John took part in a variety of equestrian competitions, gaining valuable experience. He also regularly went on the family milk round with a pony and cart, at first with his mother and then taking charge, with young Michael as the helping hand. It meant an early start to complete deliveries before school. Until the age of fourteen he was still taking part in gymkhana events, which provide great training for a child rider because of the control and balance needed, the constant jumping on and off and the fierce competitiveness. He, Steven and Michael were all good at these mounted obstacle races and would try anything – one photographer captured John and Michael standing on their ponies' backs, arms out, with no one at the animals' heads.

More formal training came from the Pony Club. John was in the Rockwood Harriers branch and a member of its eventing team. He had the smart 13.2 h.h. Mustapha, an Arab-Welsh cross, who was good at jumping, both in the show ring and across country, but not so hot at dressage. John remembers competing in the inter-branch national finals at Stoneleigh, in Warwickshire. First came the dressage test, which should be conducted in a calm, precise fashion on perfect straight lines and circles, with each new movement starting exactly at the specified marker. Mustapha had noticed the other ponies show jumping in a nearby ring and boiled over with excitement. He danced around and John forgot the test. The only bonus points he remembers picking up were the obligatory three for using a snaffle bridle. His colleagues were cross with him for piling on more than 100 penalties, but John turned the tables on them in the cross-country as the only team member to get round the course.

In his last two years in junior show jumping classes, from fourteen to sixteen, John had two ponies – Crazy Horse, who had changed hands from Mr Gregory to Jack Haigh, and Beauty. He took on both as complete novices. Crazy Horse, the elder of the two, made an encouraging start and qualified for the blue riband of novice pony jumping, the Junior Foxhunter final at Hickstead. John and his mother approached their first visit to the famous Sussex ground with awe. They decided to allow plenty of time for the 300-mile run, which involved crossing London, and set off four days before John's class. However, a series of breakdowns left them with only an hour to spare before the final when they arrived at the ground!

The All England Jumping Course was like another world to John: everything was new, from the lawn turf to the 'natural' obstacles such as the Derby Bank and ditches. Although none of the Derby features was included in the Junior Foxhunter course, Crazy Horse could see them, and his eyes popped out when he was asked to go near the ornamental lake, with its grand arrangement of rocks and shrubs. He had a refusal and a knock-down at a fence nearby. So, after a four-day journey, John's first taste of the international arena lasted little more than a minute.

The next year was John's last chance to qualify for the Leading Junior Show Jumper of the Year title at the Horse of the Year Show, Wembley. This is the goal of every teenage show jumper. Crazy Horse had reached Grade JA and so was eligible to enter the qualifiers held at county shows all over Britain. Beauty was still only five and too inexperienced to take part. John believed she would be a top class pony one day, but not before he had crossed the sixteen-year-old threshold into adult classes. John's first Wembley qualifier with Crazy Horse came at the Royal International Horse Show, then also held at the Empire Pool, Wembley. John is now renowned for controlling his nerves, but on that big day in 1971 they got the better of him. To his shame, he let the pony unseat him over one of

the huge fences. The fall cost 8 faults, though John credited
Crazy Horse with a clear round.

But the pony was not really good enough to qualify for
the Horse of the Year Show and John complained to his
mother one evening that he would never get there. He was
told, 'You certainly won't if you don't try.' The next day his
luck turned with a surprise telephone call from Mr Turner,
of Sheffield. His daughter, Victoria, was not getting on with
her pony, Little Buzzer, and John was offered the ride. The
pony was entered for several qualifiers and, after two or
three attempts, John gained a high enough placing to book
the Wembley trip. When the big day came in October, he
had to settle for a minor prize after incurring 4 faults.

Meanwhile, chasing the qualifiers took John and his
mother on a marathon tour of Britain. At the show grounds
they would bed down in the back of the horsebox in sleeping
bags. On one occasion, after John qualified at a show in
South Wales, they had no time to celebrate because the
next stop was Scotland. Mrs Whitaker drove the 450 miles
north that night, crossing the Firth of Forth Bridge at about
4.30a.m. There was no one in the kiosk to take her toll
money, so after hooting the horn and calling in vain for
attention she drove on. The lorry soon rolled into the park
venue for the show, only to be surrounded by police cars.
There had been a bank robbery just before the Whitakers
crossed the bridge and the police had received word that
their lorry had passed through without paying the toll,
making them suspects. 'They searched the lorry from top
to bottom,' recalls Mrs Whitaker. 'We had been on the road
for weeks and all they found was dirty washing.' It was the
talk of the show, causing a great deal of merriment – after
the patrol cars had gone. The irony of the situation was
magnified at the end of the day when Mrs Whitaker had to
borrow £10 from a friend as an emergency diesel kitty in
case garages on the way home to Yorkshire would not take
cheques.

Little Buzzer was an exception to the motley crew of
ponies John was usually asked to ride. He gained experience sorting out a variety of problems and built up a repu-

11

tation for getting the best out of mediocre animals. He developed a keen eye for a stride, enabling him to pick the best take-off spot, and his hands, said one commentator, would make a lace-maker weep. His parents could never afford to buy him ready-made jumpers. However, his father says that was a good thing. 'If we had bought him expensive ponies he may never have been so good. He really had to work for his success.'

By the time John finished in junior jumping he had made several friends and met the girl who was to become his wife. Social life for the teenage riders revolved around the caravans, horseboxes and stables which moved from show to show. A group of about forty youngsters were bound together by the Wembley trail. Some had successfully taken O levels, others had sewn themselves into their school uniforms for the reluctant last few weeks, but they all shared the sport and the social life that went with it.

John was a bit shy when it came to chasing girls. His mother was fairly strict and believed that plenty of sleep and no distractions were essential to competition success. John used to sneak past her with the words 'Don't be late' echoing in his ears. And if he returned to the horsebox-home after the witching hour, he had to sleep on the floor without blankets. But there was plenty of fun, especially at shows like the Royal Lancashire, near Blackpool, and Southport Flower Show, where carloads of youngsters were ferried to the fun fairs. Among John's friends were Geoff Billington and Geoff Goodwin, who have also made careers of the sport.

In spite of his mother's eagle eye and his own introvert nature, John did have one or two girlfriends. Late night strolls with girls were the unsaid part of the forays which started with 'Just going to water the ponies.'

John's first face-to-face encounter with Clare Barr came when her family went to the Whitakers' well-stocked yard to choose a pony for her young sister, Janine. Although Clare had been to some of the same shows as John, their paths had not crossed because she was interested in showing rather than jumping. It was Janine who brought the Barrs into the latter world. Clare took a fancy to John as soon as she met him, although his few words and apparent shyness meant that she had to wait for a chance of more regular contact before the relationship could develop.

Meanwhile, John was facing the difficult transition to horses. People warned him, as they did every other sixteen-year-old, that the larger animals were stronger and more clumsy because of their longer, less elastic stride. Horses were supposed to lack the cleverness that enabled ponies to get their riders out of trouble. Above all, owners would rarely trust a teenager with one of their horses until he or she had proved they could make the transition. John's parents realized they had to buy him a novice with considerable promise as the next best thing to a Grade A mount. They chose wisely and a black mare called Singing Wind came into the yard after winning one or two novice classes with Halifax lorry driver Donald Oates, who show jumped and did a bit of dealing as a hobby.

John was also fortunate in that his reputation for getting the best out of mediocre animals followed him into adult classes. John Lanni, a well-known trainer from the Doncaster area, sent John a couple of youngsters to bring on. If he had failed in the transition to senior show jumping, he would have had to fall back on helping dad with the farm. Indeed, to start with he did split his time between riding and agriculture, still driving the milk float every day. Before he could concentrate on riding John needed to make his name taking some good horses to the best known venues. Once he started winning against tough competition, more rides would start coming in, as well as useful prize money to help cover the sport's costs. The most significant development for John was the link with Mr Malcolm Barr, a director of the Wallace Arnold coach company, who had been drawn into the show world by his horse-mad daughters.

Clare and Janine had started riding as a weekend hobby, as many girls do. But instead of going off it before their teens, they became keener. Mr Barr's favourite pastime had been ocean-going yacht racing; however, as he bought better and better ponies for the girls, enabling them to graduate from hacking to the show ring, his interest grew. He found that riding was a better sport for involving the whole family and he took it up himself. He loved galloping across country, and hunting was his preferred branch of the sport. His wife, Elaine, also appreciated the fun her daughters were deriving from horses and enjoyed shows as a spectator.

Mr Barr bought a handsome chestnut hunter called Rufus the Red, which he hoped would give him good sport in the winter and have enough quality to compete in show hunter classes in the summer. Rufus landed some prizes in the show ring, but he was a disappointment in the field. 'He was super for half a day, but then you could get no more out of him,' recalls Mr Barr. He sent the horse to John for trial as a show jumper and after a few weeks John said he was too good to hunt. Rufus, a mature, well-schooled horse, made rapid progress, winning more than £260 in 1972, including a junior international trial at the Great Yorkshire Show. He was sold for a good price at the end of the season. Meanwhile Singing Wind, by the Thoroughbred stallion Sing Sing out of a hunter-jumper mare, also came on well. Her greenness and Rufus's experience complemented each other and helped John develop his talents. She qualified for the Foxhunter Championship at the Horse of the Year Show in 1972.

But not all the rides in those early days went so smoothly. To finance the expensive business of travelling to shows, a stream of animals were taken in for breaking and schooling and some were rogues. One, sent by a Halifax family, insisted on galloping flat out at jumps. John tried walking him over a pole on the ground but he would not go near any obstacle at that pace. As soon as he was pushed forward the horse launched into a gallop. So John put him in a large stable with a pole on the floor between him and his food. After a long deliberation the horse started jumping over the pole; eventually he relaxed and took it at a walk, and from that point John was able to improve his behaviour under saddle.

Another problem horse had a mouth so hard it barely responded to the bit. One day John was cantering along a lane, but the pace increased to a gallop and there was nothing he could do to stop. The lane led to a main road, John baled out and the horse kept going. It was caught two miles up the main road, none the worse for wear. John had to conquer his fear and get back on. He discovered he could prevent the horse from bolting by never giving it too much rein.

In John's first year in adult jumping his future was as uncertain as that of Clare Barr. She was at Harrogate College for Girls, studying for eight O levels. Her main hobby was showing – she qualified a 14.2 h.h. for the riding pony championship at the Horse of the Year Show – and she also enjoyed tennis.

While Rufus the Red was at the Whitakers' yard John and Clare had the occasional date. Clare took the initiative, with the help of her girl groom, Carol Nicholson, the girl-friend of Michael Carter, who drove one of the Whitaker horseboxes (by this stage John's brother Michael, was enjoying a successful run in juniors; more than one lorry could be filled with the brothers' charges and their programmes did not always coincide).

John had two good horses in Rufus and Singing Wind; however, their progress appears, with hindsight, as a prelude to the main breakthrough in his career – the discovery of Ryan's Son.

3

Ryan and Romance

In 1973 Ryan was a gawky five-year-old, whose history was
an undignified blank. His origins remained unknown until
a few years after Mr Barr bought him for John to ride. The
beginning of the story came to light at the Royal Dublin
Show, where Mr Barr was watching John compete on Ryan.
At the ringside a Mr Ned Byrne introduced himself to Mr
Barr and showed him a photograph of a mare and foal. He
claimed the foal was Ryan. Mr Barr was sceptical, but Mr
Byrne described a tiny white mark on Ryan's back in the
kidney region, invisible from the ringside or on television,
which could only be known to those with intimate knowledge of the horse.

Mr Barr took him to Ryan's stable and, sure enough, the
tell-tale spot was just as Mr Byrne had described. The
curtain covering the details of Ryan's early years was lifted.
Mr Byrne had bred him at his farm called 'The Lug' in
County Wexford, Ireland. Ryan's sire was a Thoroughbred,
Ozymandias, his dam an Irish Draught mare. Once his
Emerald Isle connection was established, he went on to win
twice the Irish Horse Board's prize for the best international horse bred on its soil.

When Ryan was four, and just broken, he was bought by
a Mrs Sandra Wright, of Denholme, near Halifax. She was
an experienced horsewoman who competed in show jumping
and eventing and enjoyed hunting through the winter.
Ryan became one of seventeen horses in her yard. Tragi-
cally, she was killed in a car crash a few years later and
with her died many memories of the young Ryan. Her
husband, Harold, remembers the hard work she put in on

the impulsive, rather awkward novice. She taught him the basics of schooling and introduced him to a variety of show jumps. To make sure he would always take natural obstacles in his stride, she practised over the walls and ditches on her farm and probably gave him a few outings with hounds.

Ryan made his early show ring forays at riding clubs in the Halifax and Keighley area and soon added to Mrs Wright's collection of rosettes. By the winter of 1972–3 she had reached two conclusions, firstly that Ryan had an abundance of jumping ability, but secondly that he was a bit too much of a handful. She believed his future lay with one of the top male riders.

One name which came to mind was that of Andrew Fielder, who had retired his famous back-kicking Vibart. He was just establishing a riding centre at Pool-in-Wharfedale and was looking for another top-class horse. Mrs Wright's father worked in the Fielders' haulage business and arranged for Andrew to try Ryan, who was a similar stamp of horse to Vibart.

The trial was a success and the Fielders agreed to buy Ryan, subject to the usual vetting. But that routine inspection led to the greatest miss of Andrew's life and left Ryan still on the market.

The vet found a curb – a lump just below the point of the hock – on each of Ryan's hind legs. He forecast that these blemishes would cause trouble and advised the Fielders against buying him. They reluctantly called off the deal. Those lumps never did cause any problems and over the years they virtually vanished.

Sandra Wright continued to jump Ryan. Her high opinion of him had been confirmed by Andrew Fielder, so she stuck out for a good price. But Ryan proved difficult to sell because his ugly conformation repelled most ringside watchers, including John. The immature Ryan had a big head, U-neck, saucepan feet, long back and angular rump. However, John's father saw through these superficial drawbacks. 'I liked the way he walked and put his feet down. He looked

17

like a milk horse, but his cockiness set him off.' But the price was beyond Mr Whitaker's means.

He had discussed Ryan's potential with Donald Oates, who was always interested in doing a bit of horse dealing. He took up the bargaining and Mrs Wright let him ride Ryan at one or two shows. Mr Oates managed to argue the price down and bought Ryan; meanwhile Mr Whitaker remained intent on getting the horse. How John came to have the ride is a painful story for Mr Oates. He had entered Ryan in the usual set of novice classes, but because he was suffering from piles he was forced to stand down and offer his place to John. It took about three jumps in the collecting ring to convince John that this was the best horse he had ever sat on. He won two firsts and a second in a week; but these prize-winning rounds awoke others to Ryan's potential, and the same problem for the Whitakers remained: the price.

The solution arose from John's success the previous season with Mr Barr's ex-hunter, Rufus the Red. Mr Barr had enjoyed the experience of owning a winning horse and he had great faith in John's ability. He decided that it would be only fair to plough back the money gained on Rufus into a replacement. The 1973 season got underway and one or two animals were considered but ruled out as not good enough or too expensive.

Then John had that chance ride on Ryan and immediately swung to his father's view of the horse's potential. Mr Whitaker decided it was time to mention Ryan to Mr Barr.

John took Mr Barr to see Ryan at Donald Oates's yard in Halifax. Despite Ryan's ungainly appearance, Mr Barr was instantly won over by his personality and his sang froid at all that went on around him. He also seemed to jump decently! The deal was struck at £2,500, with the Whitakers paying twenty per cent, £500, as a token of their faith in the horse. Ryan was not a cheap novice; because of his appearance he would have been worth little as a hunter had he failed as a show jumper.

Ryan proved to be a good horse straightaway. He had a huge jump and if he touched a pole he gave the rest of the course a foot of daylight. He listened to John's commands, always tried and only refused when the alternative was to attempt the impossible and hurt himself. His only drawback was that he was headstrong and became very difficult to control if he was too fresh. Within three months with John, Ryan won nearly £200, moving from Grade C to Grade B. It was already clear that he was that rare combination, a careful horse with bags of scope. Harvey Smith's description of him was spot on: 'A carthorse with a Thoroughbred engine.'

While John was getting to know Ryan, Clare Barr was busy passing eight O levels. The occasional date was fitted in, with Michael Carter getting John out of the Whitaker nest to make up a foursome with Clare and Carol. Clare's academic success meant she was an A-level and university candidate and she went into the lower sixth form at the Harrogate school. But it was her love of horses and interest in John that kept growing as she passed her seventeenth birthday. Her desire to stay at school waned and she left in the summer of 1974 to go to work with horses at the Whitaker yard. She knuckled down to the stable chores, taking a special interest in Ryan, and travelled to all the shows with John and one of his parents.

In those early days John worked hard to curb Ryan's over-exuberance. Instead of using a severe bit, he schooled the horse for hours at home, using draw reins for extra control and to bring Ryan's head and neck into the correct position. The effort paid off. Ryan upgraded to A early in 1974, giving John a chance to pit himself against Britain's top riders.

He hit the show jumping heights in July at the Great Yorkshire Show, in Harrogate. On the first day both Ryan and Singing Wind had several fences down in very disappointing rounds. On the way home John hung his head and said he was out of his depth against the likes of Harvey Smith, David Broome and Caroline Bradley. But his father said he should have another go – after all, the entries were paid for.

The next day was like a dream come true. He won two

19

classes, one on each horse, and Ryan's victory came in the day's main class, the Midland Bank Championship. The £300 prize was his first three-figure win. After that he never looked back, landing prizes at all the major shows. He made his first trip to Wembley in the autumn for the Courvoisier Championships, where he won a class. That winter saw his debut on the continent, at Zuidlaren, in Holland. After that Ryan jumped for his country a record number of times. From 1975 to 1982, inclusive, he made twenty-eight appearances for the British team, jumping twenty-nine clear rounds, including nine double clears in Nations Cups.

In 1975 it was important for John to consolidate his position among the top flight of British competitors, so that he would be able to compete at this country's major events, like the Royal International and Horse of the Year shows, and be in line for selection for British teams. He achieved both ambitions, wearing the Union Jack on his saddle cloth at Dinard, Vienna and Poland's international show.

But the next season brought a bitter mixture of triumph and disappointment. It was 1976, the year of the Montreal Olympics. John, then twenty, and eight-year-old Ryan looked certain to be chosen for the British team. They won an Olympic trial at Cardiff, were highly placed in two other trials and at two testing international shows at Aachen and Lucerne. The selectors told John to wrap Ryan in cotton wool ready for the trans-Atlantic trip. But then, out of the blue, they announced a final trial at Hickstead – usually a happy stamping ground for Ryan, but not this time.

Ryan was rushed to the event from his enforced holiday and lack of work made him ominously headstrong. In the ring he behaved like a lunatic, stopping several times, leaping about and dancing sideways to evade John's commands. The pair were dropped from the team. John was disappointed – the prospect of going to the Olympics had been a thrill for him – but he was not surprised at the selectors' decision following Ryan's poor performance. In the back of his mind he knew the horse was not yet ready for such a severe test. His father was more upset because of the way John had been misled. Afterwards Ryan went from strength to strength, becoming that season's top money winner with more than £10,000 on his card. He won the National Championship at Hickstead and came equal third in the Jumping Derby, hammering home the irony of his failure in Hickstead's international arena earlier in the summer.

His successes made it easier for people to criticize the selectors for leaving John out of the Olympic team. But John was not bitter. He knew that on the day it had been a difficult decision and it was predictable that Ryan's refusals would put them off. However, he also took delight in the fact that Ryan's blossoming talent subsequently proved them wrong. All Ryan's connections now see it as a blessing that the horse did not go to Montreal. He was spared a gruelling test while he was still inexperienced and yet to reach his peak. Also, conditions at Montreal were imperfect, with a huge course for the individual contest made worse by torrential rain.

In contrast to the peaks and troughs of Olympic year, 1977 was rather an anti-climax. John and Ryan stayed in the top flight, but there were no spectacular wins and much less prize money rolled in. One of the reasons was Ryan's waistline. He had been overfed through the winter and remained on the fat side for jumping. He is what is known as a good doer, staying well covered on little food.

The New Year brought a strange mixture of romantic pleasure and appalling worry. The centre of the romance was, of course, Clare. She and John announced their engagement in January 1978, about three and a half years after Clare had gone to live and work at the Whitakers.

But their domestic happiness was soon rocked with worry over Ryan's health. During his winter rest he came in from the field slightly lame. There was heat in his off hind hoof and it was thought a bit of gravel had worked its way into the wall of his foot. But instead of responding to treatment, his condition deteriorated. It was decided his hoof would have to be X-rayed and examined by a specialist. John,

21

Clare and Mr Barr took him to the Equine Research Station, at Newmarket.

They waited uneasily for the results of the X-ray. At last the veterinary surgeon came out with a cheerful face, saying it would be an easy thing to cure. 'There were thousands of cases like this in the First World War,' he told them. Ryan had broken off the tip of the pedal bone at the base of his foot. Luckily the vulnerable navicular bone was unharmed. The injury was like those caused to horses in the 1914–18 War by specially-laid traps comprising a spike in a hole, camouflaged by foliage. Ryan's fracture must have been similarly caused by treading on something hard and sharp. The detached slice of bone had to be removed under general anaesthetic and they were warned that about one in four hundred horses died inexplicably on the operating table. However, it was Ryan's only chance of recovery, so the extraction went ahead. It was a complete success and he soon regained his soundness. The sliver of bone, nearly an inch square, is now bottled as a souvenir. Ryan has never been lame since and, as John says, 'It's a good job he's got big feet.'

Ryan proved his 100 per cent recovery by giving John his best season to date in 1978. John won the Cock o' the North Championship at the Great Yorkshire and had victories at Hickstead and the Horse of the Year Show, where he won the Service spurs for the best overall performance during the week at Wembley. This prize is a replica of the spurs won by the Black Prince, son of Edward III, at the battle of Crécy in France in 1346. Ryan finished the season with nearly £17,000 prize money.

Again Ryan followed a year of supremacy with a quieter season, although John was still leading rider at both the Birmingham International Show and Olympia and had wins at Hickstead and Dortmund, West Germany. However, the real highlight of 1979 was John and Clare's autumn wedding.

Since the pair had started dating seven years earlier Clare had never gone out with another man. At first they had only had horses in common and it took a determined effort by Clare to get to know John better. He was a typical Yorkshireman, a man of few words, unintentional master of understatement, apprehensive of showing emotion or revealing his views. He had taken little interest in being educated, but Clare soon found he had his wits about him and that he saw a great deal more than he commented on. His humour was of the 'dry Martini' variety, always ready to poke fun – at himself as well as others.

They complemented each other, Clare being the more positive character, quick to draw conclusions and less placid when it came to taking life's knocks. John was easy going – anything for a quiet life. But he was never weak willed – that would have lost Clare's respect. When he set his heart on something he was immovably stubborn and, without putting anyone's back up, he tended to get his own way on the few issues that he felt mattered.

In the year leading up to the marriage they were based at Clare's home, near Harrogate. Family relations were cemented as they had been during Clare's stay with the Whitakers. Mr Barr had realized soon after Clare left school that she was 'hell-bent on marrying John' and he was content at the prospect. Mr Barr enjoyed the association with sporting success, but he was also pleased to play a part in bringing John's natural gifts to fruition. He saw in John an unusual combination of natural horsemanship and an ability to compete.

During the engagement an extra girl was brought in to look after John's horses, enabling Clare to turn her mind to home building. The couple found an old farmhouse perched on the edge of the Pennines, with eight acres of land and a motley assortment of outbuildings. The winter after the marriage was spent making the most of a bleak location. By spring 1980 their first baby was on the way, and a new stable block was being built to house the growing number of horses that John was offered to ride.

In the late 1970s another factor which contributed to John's rise up the show-jumping ladder was a succession of good second horses. At first Singing Wind filled this spot, but she was owned by his parents and John needed to start attracting rides from other owners. Golden Vale, owned by Mr Rose, of the Bericote stud, was one of the the first to fill this bill, taking the pressure off Ryan. Others completed the equestrian team by competing in novice or speed classes.

John always tried every animal that was offered. It didn't matter what the horse's reputation was, how little he knew about the owner or how far he had to travel. Good horses came out of the blue, from chance phone calls. John never worried about a horse's breeding or appearance – Ryan had taught him that handsome is as handsome does. Looking round the show jumping world he could see that top horses came in all shapes and sizes. He developed a versatile riding style, always adapting himself to the horse and never imposing a single pattern. The jumpers varied in length of stride, in the strength of the hold they took on the bit, in boldness and in their capacity for mischief. Although he was still a young rider, his experience on a variety of ponies as a child, including difficult ones, continued to reap its reward.

John was established in the top flight in 1978 and 1979, but there were still half a dozen professionals ahead of him who took priority for team selection when it came to the major international championships. In those two years Britain fielded its most successful team ever – David Broome, Caroline Bradley, Malcolm Pyrah and Derek Ricketts – to win World and European Championships. But they were all professionals and, as Olympic year loomed, the selectors once again had to turn their attention to the country's young amateurs.

4

Top of the Tree

John was an obvious contender for Britain's Olympic team in 1980. This time the selectors were so keen for him to go that they arranged for him to ride Anglezarke – then owned by Trevor Banks – in the early part of the season to give a second string to his bow. Ryan soon proved that he was on top form and became as firmly established on the equine short-list as John was on the riders'.

But politics overtook the event after Russia invaded Afghanistan and the British government urged all competitors to boycott the Moscow Games. Equestrianism was one of the few sports to take any notice. John had mixed feelings about the British Show Jumping Association's decision to abide by the government's wishes. He was desperately keen to go to the Olympics, especially after his last-minute disappointment in 1976. He also knew that Ryan, then twelve, was in his prime and would give him a good chance of a medal. Despite all the prize money and titles that had become available to show jumpers, John's number one ambition remained the traditional one of every sportsman – to win an Olympic gold medal. He was not a political person and had no strong feelings about the Russian invasion, but he did believe that the government knew best on the issue and that it had the authority to influence people competing for their country.

Fortunately all the top show jumping nations took the same decision and the International Equestrian Federation was able to organize a 'Substitute Olympics' at Rotterdam. John had competed at the Dutch show before and the programme included a range of international classes for which the riders could take two or three horses. But when it came to the size of the fences for the Olympic-style team and individual championships, the resemblance to an ordinary international show ended. The courses were the biggest John had faced.

The British team was the all-amateur foursome who would have gone to Moscow: John, Nick Skelton, Graham Fletcher and Tim Grubb. For the team championship chef d'équipe Ronnie Massarella showed his faith in twenty-five-year-old John by asking him to go last. In each of the two rounds the best three scores counted towards the total, so the fourth rider in could make a crucial difference.

Clears were few and far between and of John's team-mates only Nick Skelton on Maybe was without fault in the first round. Graham Fletcher had 8 faults on Preachan, and Tim Grubb had a refusal with Night Murmur, as well as fences down, for a total of 14¼ faults. That was the score which the team needed to discard and John responded with a clear, which put Britain among the leaders, Canada and Austria being the main rivals. In the second round Graham Fletcher had 8 again, and Nick Skelton returned one of the competition's few double clears. Tim Grubb got a considerable improvement from his horse for 6½ faults. Another clear from John would have clinched gold, two fences down would drop the team to bronze. He hit one, and so Britain won the team silver, behind Canada and ahead of Austria. West Germany, the United States, Switzerland and France were in their wake and three of the thirteen teams did not complete the event. Britain's team of amateurs had done themselves proud against the best of the world's riders.

For the individual championship the course was even bigger. Several of the early riders came out of the arena on foot because their horses had fallen – an unusual sight in show jumping. Nick Skelton was the first British rider to go and Ronnie Massarella said he could retire if he wanted to. Nick took on the challenge and, although he had a couple of fences down, he made the course look easier. Ryan, who was jumping out of his skin, just tipped one pole in the first round before jumping clear in the second. No competitor managed a double clear, so John, Hugo Simon from Austria and Melanie Smith from the USA, each on a total of 4, had to jump off for the medals.

The deciding round was against the clock, so the luck of the draw played a part. Melanie Smith, on Calypso, went first and had 4 faults in a fairly good time. John had to cut a few corners, both to beat her and to present a tough target for Hugo Simon on the chestnut flyer, Gladstone. Sadly John had one fence down, although his time was faster than Melanie's. Hugo set out for a slow clear; had he hit a fence he would have left John in the gold medal position, but his gamble came off and he clinched victory despite having a time fault.

John's double silver medal made Rotterdam Britain's best Olympic performance at show jumping. Never before had medals been won in both team and individual competitions. The only disappointment was that removing the contest from the Games proper had detracted from their value. Afterwards John felt slightly irritated that his medals were not quite the real thing. But he also knew that on a different day, at a different place, he might have come home empty handed. Remembering the size of the obstacles, he knew it had been a true Olympic test.

It was a successful year on all fronts for John. He and Clare had settled into their new home and were between them managing the numerous jobs associated with travelling a show jumping team. Clare filled in the entry forms and did the books, John trained the horses and did various jobs around the farm. Between them they managed the yard, employing one girl groom. In June their first child, Louise Sarah, was born, fulfilling another wish, because both John and Clare were keen to have a family.

In the ring John's victories included the Grand Prix at Wales and the West and a major class at Aachen, one of Europe's toughest international shows. In the Jumping Derby at Hickstead, shortly after the Substitute Olympics, John came within an inch of joining his brother, Michael, in what would have been a historic jump-off. The Derby has rarely produced two clear rounds, let alone by two related competitors. Michael, who was only twenty, riding Owen Gregory, triumphed with the only clear; John rolled a pole off the very last jump after clearing all the bogey fences. John's equal second in that high-value competition helped him to attain a total, on Ryan, of more than £26,400 for the season, making him top money winner for the third time. However, it was not only Ryan who was winning for John; his second horse, Rushgreen, formerly ridden by Ann Smith, also landed plenty of prizes at national and international shows.

John and Ryan were now on a par with the top professional combinations and this was recognized by their inclusion in Britain's teams for the European Championships at Munich in 1981 and the World Championships at Dublin in 1982. John had proved he could withstand the extra pressure of jumping for his country and Ryan had maintained remarkable consistency. As the generation of horses in the 1978 world-beating team, which included Tigre, Hydrophane Coldstream, Law Court and Philco, passed their prime, Ryan moved up into the top four.

1981 started with a taste of the sort of courses that might characterize the Los Angeles Olympics in 1984. At the World Cup final at Baltimore, in the United States, the course builder was Bertalan de Nemethy, the US team coach who would later be chosen to build the Olympic obstacles. The main problem, apart from the size of the fences, was the distances between them. The course-building ploy of using unconventional distances, which are not multiples of normal canter strides, is designed to test the rider's ability to control the horse, making him shorten or lengthen stride to arrive at the right take-off point. At Baltimore some horses fell because they were wrong at very difficult fences. One or two riders complained but John appreciated that some good course-building ideas were being developed. He and Ryan stayed upright, although they were not among the top prize winners.

The European Championships were held at Munich in September. With John in the team were Malcolm Pyrah,

28

David Broome and Liz Edgar. It turned out to be Malcolm Pyrah's show, with Towerlands Anglezarke the best of the British horses. He jumped a double clear in the team championship, won by West Germany, and landed the silver medal in the individual championship, behind Paul Schockemöhle on Deister. Ryan was the second best team horse with a clear, and 8 faults. He was also well placed in the final leg of the individual, but a poor performance in the opening speed class relegated him to sixteenth place overall.

John's second horse, Askern, owned by John Massarella, was also well placed. His performance was some consolation for John losing his previous second-string mount, Rushgreen, who had died of grass sickness. This tragedy, striking a perfectly healthy horse, was a reminder of how fickle show jumping fortunes could be. No matter how great his success, John realized that ill luck could wipe it out overnight. Horses could go lame or die or just become stale without warning.

As if acknowledging that fate was at least partly beyond his control, John built up small superstitions around competitions. Parts of a bridle associated with victory were kept in use until they were worn out almost to the point of danger. Returning to a show where he had previously enjoyed success, he liked to warm up in the same part of the collecting ring.

At the Horse of the Year show in 1981 Ryan passed the £100,000 mark for winnings in his Grade A career. It was the cumulative total of seven seasons' jumping. The following year started well, with John winning a bronze medal at the World Cup final in Gothenberg, Sweden. He was the only British rider to win a medal in the first six years of this event.

For the World Championships at Dublin in June the selectors chose nearly the same team as the previous year. The only difference was that Liz Edgar and Everest Forever were replaced by their colleagues, Nick Skelton and Everest If Ever. John helped the team to a bronze medal, with the second best performance by a British competitor. He had

29

three fences down over the three rounds, which included a jump-off with the West Germans for the silver medal. Once again Malcolm Pyrah with Anglezarke returned the best British score, with just one fence down. He went on to win the individual silver medal after having to ride three other horses; in the world championship the top four competitors ride each other's horses in the final deciding leg. It was Norbert Koof from West Germany who did best on his rivals' mounts to take the gold. In the individual John was well down the order going into the third and final leg because of a mediocre round in the first phase, a speed class. He was half-hearted about the final contest – not the right frame of mind for a huge course which needed attacking. He got into trouble at a combination, Ryan refused and he retired.

But Ryan finished the season well, winning a total of about £35,000, a figure only bettered by Anglezarke. However, after Ryan's uncharacteristic performance at Dublin, one or two of the selectors formed the opinion that he was beginning to show his age. It was assumed he had reached his peak in 1980 and that by 1982, at fourteen, he was beginning a downward trend. This opinion was to play a part in dealing John the worst blow of his career when, in 1983, he was initially left out of the British team for the European Championships at Hickstead. He classed this as worse than being dropped from the Montreal Olympics and it made his subsequent medal-winning – after his last-minute inclusion because of injury to a team horse – all the more sweet.

The events of 1983, one of John's best seasons, will be recounted in detail in a later chapter, because they formed the first steps towards the Olympics at Los Angeles. It was the year which restored Ryan as Britain's top money winner and took John to the top of the riders' league. The rankings, worked out by computer, are based on a rider's winnings on all Grade A horses. John's high position showed he had reached the top of the tree in his own right, not just as Ryan's partner.

In each of the major championships from 1980 to 1983

John rode a different second horse. The ill-fated Rushgreen was the first, followed by Askern, Betsy and Charles Newton's Charlie's Angel and Fred Brown's Saint Mungo. The variety was proof both of John's horsemanship and of the strength in depth of his stable. His growing string of Grade As meant he could keep up a full programme of county shows, national championships and jumping abroad, without forcing Ryan to compete every week. After 1980 John was able to jump Ryan less and save him for the big occasions. This paid off – literally – because he won more money in fewer outings. Ryan's sustained period at the top was partly due to John's policy of never overjumping him. It was thanks to the other horses, and their several owners, that the pressure was taken off Ryan.

Another factor behind this change in tempo was Ryan's mellowing temperament. In his youth he would always become very headstrong after a rest; it would take two or three shows for him to calm down and John would need to give him plenty of schooling at home. In his teens Ryan settled down and could come out near his best after a period away from the show ring. Indeed, his performance at a big occasion benefited from the extra freshness. So he continued to have at least two months off in the winter, starting his spring campaign at the indoor World Cup final. Then May and June would be taken quietly before building up to the year's major international events.

On the winter indoor circuit, including qualifiers for the World Cup, John's main horse was Clonee Temple. Like Charlie's Angel she was owned by Mr and Mrs Newton, from County Durham. Clonee Temple, a chestnut mare, developed as an indoor specialist because she hated jumping water – a regular feature in outdoor arenas. If she saw a water jump in the ring, she would be put off her stride for all the fences just through worrying about it. Strangely enough, when water was occasionally included indoors she flew over it, her confidence undisturbed. All horses have different characters and both John and Clare take delight in getting to know each of the individuals in their yard.

31

5

At Home

PART I: BEHIND THE SCENES

The journey to John Whitaker's home takes you from the traffic-fuming A629, near Huddersfield, to a remote small-holding set on top of rolling Yorkshire hills. At first glance one of Britain's most important show jumping yards could be any northern farm, with its stone and slate house and irregular collection of outbuildings. But look across the field and the height of the practice jumps gives a clue that this is a champion's base.

The house and stable yard nestle together just below the lane, which acts as a bit of a break against winds off the Pennines. From the drive you can see half a dozen handsome horses looking over stable doors, among them the large, dark bay head of John's favourite, Ryan's Son, with his familiar white blaze and cocky look. Everyone uses the back door and you get a great welcome from a shaggy little terrier called Mindy.

John is about thirty, stands about 5 feet 7 inches and weighs 10 stone. You can tell he is a grafter by the weather-beaten face, broad shoulders and worker's hands. His clothes are chosen for comfort and to stand wear – vanity does not come into it. Were it not for the rows of rosettes on the kitchen wall and the prize bottles of champagne in the living room, you would guess he was a farmer. And that is his official job when it comes to registering as an amateur show jumper. He is also a family man; he and Clare have two children – Louise, born in June 1980, and Robert, born in January 1983.

Sheltered below the stone farmhouse lies a modern L-shaped block of spacious stables, enclosing a spotless yard. Two large metal horseboxes are parked in the middle, one with the swish grey and burgundy livery of John's sponsors, the Next fashion shop company. At the far end a long caravan is home for the girl grooms and, behind that, wooden outbuildings have been converted to provide an extra half dozen stables.

Fifteen horses look over the half doors, some of them with wavy manes from yesterday's show plaits. Each is rugged up to keep its coat short and glossy. Beds of wood shavings are stacked high round the walls to protect thousands of pounds worth of show jumping legs from knocks. The horses eat from fixed mangers and get their water from automatic dispensers operated by their tongues – these save the girls lugging buckets to and fro.

The tack room boasts a wallful of competition saddles, with the special show jumping adaptations of a deep seat, spring tree and forward-cut flaps with knee rolls, which allow the leather to mould itself round the rider's legs. Bridles are decorated with brass studs and equipped with running martingales, the rider's best friend when it comes to keeping his mount's head low and steady on the approach to a fence. Ten different types of bit, mostly varieties of snaffle, point to the hands of a master and perfectionism in choosing the means of control. The travelling bandages are stretched and faded, conjuring up images of thousands of miles on the road to reach shows spanning two continents, from Vienna to Los Angeles. Racks are piled high with rugs to cater for the horse's every need, from sweat-covered flanks heaving after the Hickstead Derby to winter coddling of the clipped horse.

Despite the trend to year-round show jumping as the winter indoor circuit expanded, the main season still spans the summer, with its traditional highlights of county shows and national and international championships. It starts indoors with spring shows at every region's best covered arenas. As April turns to May, show organizers take the outdoor plunge and the programme runs through rain and shine until the habitual move back inside for pre-Wembley shows and then the real climax at the Horse of the Year Show, Wembley. The Christmas show at Olympia is one of the few additions to the calendar to attract the same sentiment as the vintage events.

Preparations for the season start in February after Ryan's Son and John's other top horses have enjoyed a well-earned rest. Their coats are long, manes and tails are bushy, and they have enjoyed frequent rolls in the mud. It is not much consolation for the groom, struggling with the matted hair, to know that this is a horse's natural way of adding an extra layer of insulation against the elements.

When the horses are brought in from grass they keep their teddy bear coats through the first fortnight of roadwork. The inevitable sweating speeds up the fittening process and clears the fur. As the exercise is stepped up, too much sweat would lead to unwanted weight loss and, with the first show only a few weeks away, it is time to convert the mudlarks into smart public performers.

John's wife, Clare, supervises this transformation and rolls up her sleeves to help with the work. Her teenage experience of showing taught her how to bring out the best in a horse's appearance. She sets about the shaggy coats with the clippers, guiding the blades against the lie of the hair and taking care not to make any lines with the edges. The most spectacular change comes as long feathers are sheared from the fetlocks, just above the hooves, leaving even Ryan's legs looking sleek and streamlined. She pulls the manes into fine, flat fringes short enough for show plaits, and the tops of the tails are transformed from lavatory brushes to the neatly tapering shape which shows off the horse's quarters.

Daughter Louise is fascinated by all this activity. Whatever Mum does to the show jumpers, she copies on her tiny Shetland pony, Bo Bo. If one of the short-toothed pulling combs goes missing, it is a fair bet that Louise will be trying to drag it through Bo Bo's mop. She has to stand on a plastic bottle crate to reach all the way up his neck – and from that height it is a small step to climb aboard.

But Clare's time in the stable yard is limited and the three girls, whom she trained, can cope with virtually all the tasks. These days her other duties are even more pressing. As well as caring single-handed for two children and a large house, she has to shop and cook for up to six adults, tend the garden, fill in entry forms, do the book keeping, send off bills and cheques, take Louise to play school, answer the phone, order horse feed . . . .

The administration of the show programme and the arrangements with various owners does not stop at the string of established Grade As which John takes to the most prestigious events. A second string of up-and-coming horses is ridden by John's young deputy, Alan Fazakerley. Alan was born in 1963 in Salford, an industrial suburb of Manchester made famous through Lowry's paintings. He did not touch a horse until he was six, but he inherited a yen to ride from his mother, who had always wished to work with horses. He learnt the basics of show jumping on ponies and left school at sixteen intent on making a career of the sport. Within two years he had joined John's stable. Now he takes on tough competition at provincial shows, where the average weekend show jumper would be way out of his depth.

The up-and-coming brigade includes show jumpers at every stage of development, from raw novices to horses in their first full season at Grade A. The British Show Jumping Association measures a horse's progress by the amount of prize money it has won at shows affiliated to the organization. In 1985 the bands were: up to £299 grade C; from £300 to £799 grade B; £800 and over grade A. The figures are revised most years to take account of rising prize money. Within each grade there are horses with quite a range of experience and there are a variety of classes to take account of this and to change the type of entertainment on offer to spectators.

John prefers to bring on his horses from scratch. The advantages are that he can influence their progress before they have formed jumping habits and before any other rider has put his stamp on the animal. Novices also cost less and their value nearly always goes up, which is far better for the ego as well as for business. Getting on to a Grade A automatically means that his riding will be compared with his predecessor's and it can be quite a responsibility taking on an expensive animal. The advantage is that a Grade A has proved itself and John has enjoyed 'taking over' rides on some excellent horses, including Rushgreen and Askern and, more recently, Charlie's Angel and San Salvador.

Ryan is a prime example of a horse that was nurtured from the start by John and his team of helpers. Following in the great horse's footsteps are three others that have risen from novice to premier league in his hands. One of these is the magnificent grey stallion, Novilheiro. He is an Andalusian, bred in Portugal for bull-fighting. Fortunately he was never used for this purpose and it took a few years to discover in which field he would shine.

He was brought to England at the age of five, in 1977, by a Frenchman who makes his living here as a freelance instructor. Jean-Phillipe Giacomini, who is still part-owner of the horse with the Whitakers, started him on a dressage career. Novilheiro got part way up the grades, in a sport which is the equestrian equivalent of ballet, before being tried over fences. He showed promise, and international rider Rachel Bayliss took him eventing, which combined his dressage training with cross-country and show jumping. But he was not quite fast enough and treated the solid hunting-style obstacles with too much respect. It was then, when the horse was eight and approaching his prime, that John got the chance to turn him into a show jumper.

Novilheiro's thorough schooling for dressage had already trained him to combine power with obedience and balance. Thanks to that he sailed up through the show jumping grades in a matter of months and in 1981 the Whitakers bought a half share in him. Over the next two years he became a top class horse, in with a good chance of winning every time out. His winnings in 1983 totalled £12,582, plus a car, and he was runner-up in the league for horses with most winnings in competitions under national rules.

As a stallion he leads a double life, alternating show

ring performances with stud duties. He serves about fifteen mares during the spring and early summer. An impressive demonstration of his versatility was given one year during Royal Show week at Stoneleigh. John had planned to leave him at home for a rest, but then Ted Edgar rang up to ask if he would bring him to cover a mare at his Everest Stud a few miles from the show ground. The mare was duly served on the second day of the show while Ryan's Son was on duty in the show ring. But the next day, in sweltering heat, John decided to give his old campaigner a rest and instead saddled Novilheiro for the main class. He won it, leaving the country's best in his wake. Novilheiro's reward was another mating with Ted Edgar's mare.

At home Novilheiro is usually a perfect gentleman both to groom and ride, although he is more easily excited than the others when a strange horse enters the yard. The sight of Louise's pony will set him pacing round his box and whinnying and, if he catches a glimpse of one of his mates in the paddock, his squealing calls soon split the usually calm atmosphere. However, the extra aggression in his stallion nature can never quite be trusted. Like other horses he will sometimes flatten his ears and aim a mock bite during grooming. But one summer's day he went too far with this game and struck head groom Angie Padfield with his teeth, cracking two ribs.

Two younger horses, groomed to replace Ryan in international classes, are Saint Mungo and Hopscotch, both chestnuts. Mungo, born in 1974, was John's back-up horse for the Olympics at Los Angeles because he had not only scope, but also a calm, brave temperament. He was bred in Cumbria; his sire, Bilsborough, was a Thoroughbred and his dam, Ruby's Daughter, a Thoroughbred-Clydesdale cross. He belongs to one of John's most enthusiastic backers, Mr Fred Brown, who has an agricultural machinery business in Otley.

Mr Brown had become interested in show jumping through his daughter, Gill, who had ridden since she was a child. He was on the look out for a good young horse for her when Saint Mungo caught his eye at the Horse of the

Year Show in 1981. He was being ridden by Susan Jay, from London, in the Foxhunter Championship, the blue riband event for novices, who had come through two qualifying rounds to reach the Wembley final. Like many other ringside watchers, Mr Brown was doing a bit of talent spotting among these up-and-coming young horses. He liked the look of Mungo, although he won no prize, and put a mark by his name in the catalogue. But when he came to negotiate a price with the girl's father he kept being outbid by other interested parties. By the end of the show week the price had doubled and Mr Brown said, 'You can keep it.'

An old man who had noticed Mr Brown's disappointment at the way things had gone came up and told him that he could buy Mungo's full brother at the breeder John Dickinson's yard in Cumbria. Mr Brown and Gill went to see the dark brown six-year-old. They took to him straightaway and bought him on the 'rebound' from missing out on Mungo – he is called Rebound to mark the occasion. He joined Gill's two Grade As to give her an extra ride in novice classes and the satisfaction of schooling an unspoiled youngster.

While Gill was getting on famously with her new horse, Mr Brown was unexpectedly given a second chance to buy Saint Mungo. Mr Jay, who was still the owner, came up to Mr Brown and said he could have the horse after all. But as Mr Brown knew that Mungo had just refused in the ring, he wanted to think about it and let Gill try the horse first. They went to see Mungo at the Jays' yard, liked him and thought this time the deal was on. But the Jays were attached to the horse and said they wanted to win just one more class before parting with him. The saga dragged on again until the end of the season, when Gill was jumping Rebound at Wembley in the Godfrey Davis Grade C Championship. It was the last time she rode competitively as she had decided to retire on a high note and concentrate on her career. She also felt her father would have just as much fun out of show jumping if his horses were ridden by someone like John Whitaker – an old friend of the family as well as a top-class rider. Both Mungo and Rebound are registered with the BSJA as owned by Gill – now Mrs G. W. Rhodes.

John tried out Mungo before Mr Brown finally clinched the deal at the 1982 Horse of the Year Show, exactly a year after his first rebuff. Gill never rode Mungo at a show, but she did set to work on him at home to improve his flat work – his head was too high, his back rigid, his stride too long and inflexible and his hindquarters not active enough. He was also strong and inclined to pull. While Gill laid the foundations for his improvement at home, John's deputy rider, Alan Fazakerley, rode Mungo at shows. The horse was Grade B and needed plenty of small classes to develop his improved homework into polished performances in the ring. Alan was also riding Rebound, who reached Grade A before Mungo, despite being a year younger.

By a strange coincidence, another rising star in John's yard, Hopscotch, first made his mark in the 1981 Foxhunter final, on the day when Mungo caught Mr Brown's eye. Hopscotch, then only five, won the championship, so rewarding a year of careful training by both John and Alan, as he had risen from nil winnings to Grade B. He is a German-bred horse, but more finely built than the typical powerhouse variety that most West German riders use. In fact, he would not look out of place in a show hunter class.

Hopscotch reached Grade A in 1982 and for the rest of that season and in 1983 he was slowly introduced to tougher classes. He was often ridden by Alan, who followed a circuit of provincial shows second only in prestige to the international and richest national classes which John and the other top-ranked riders pursued. He won several of the aptly named 'Talentspotters' competitions specially designed for horses new to Grade A.

John gained the same pleasure from seeing Hopscotch blossom as he had all those years before with his little pony, Bonnie. Like Bonnie, Hopscotch had come into his hands as a novice, completely unknown on the show circuit. Also like Bonnie, he had joined the cream of his generation and his value had increased tenfold in a year. Of course,

Hopscotch was not for sale. Both John and Clare were glad that he and some of the other horses were their own and so completely under their control. Not all owners are as loyal as Mr Brown, who regards John and Clare as part of the family and whose daughter, Gill, is godmother to Louise Whitaker.

Two of John's other Grade As show his versatility as a rider: the one with the look of a racehorse about him is San Salvador, bred in Argentina and owned by a South African, Mrs Sheila Grayston. San Salvador had crossed the world twice, from America to Africa and back, before John got the ride in 1983. The horse was very careful and could put in a stop if he was at all worried about a fence. John at first picked small courses for him to build up his confidence. He soon proved a winner, being one of the fastest horses against the clock that John had ridden.

By contrast Vesper's Son, a Shire cross Thoroughbred, is built like a tank. When he first arrived at the Whitaker stable after a long spell at grass he was not the most popular of rides because legs spread-eagled across his huge barrel soon started aching. Even those used to riding several horses a day were stiff after riding Vesper. When he arrived early in 1984 no one would have believed that the long-haired, cumbersome creature was a Grade A who had enjoyed some success before having the previous season off. Clare and the grooms set about him with the clippers and pulling comb. Once slimmed down by hours of roadwork, he began to win favour because of his kind nature and surprisingly scopey jump.

Compared with him, San Salvador felt like a Shetland, but John was used to adapting his style to suit the horse. This is harder than it looks and John runs through a careful mental routine to make sure he gives each horse what it needs rather than a rehash of the way he rode the last one. He clears his mind of all the thoughts associated with his previous ride and works out just what he wants from the next horse and how best to achieve it. He remembers a season when Ryan had not gone quite so well in some

'The photographer wanted something different...' so John (right, aged about 13) and Michael obliged during the Greenhead Park Show at Huddersfield

Above: John, 14, riding Mustapha on the cross country course at the Pony Club championships, Stoneleigh

Left: John at 17, on one of his first good horses, Singing Wind

Below: There were times when Donald Whitaker had to get on Silver to straighten him up – this was one of them

Above: John and Ryan's Son making their breakthrough at the Great Yorkshire Show in 1974

Below: The winning British Nations Cup team at Hickstead in 1977. From the left: Derek Ricketts on Hydrophane Coldstream, John on Ryan's Son, Tony Newbery on Warwick and the late Caroline Bradley on Marius

The fences were certainly of Olympic dimensions at the 1980 'Substitute Games' for show jumpers in Rotterdam, where John and Ryan's Son took two silver medals

The silver-medal winning team at Rotterdam. From the left: Tim Grubb, Nick Skelton, John Whitaker, Graham Fletcher and chef d'équipe Ronnie Massarella

competitions because his riding was being influenced by two very strong horses, who had blunted his responses.

Just as horses vary tremendously to ride, their characters are as diverse as those of humans. Vesper is a softy, a gentle giant. But San Salvador is nervous and, if frightened, can lash out or bite. Being a Thoroughbred, Salvador has a fine coat and sensitive skin and he is rather ticklish to groom. Clare realized his bad temper was partly due to worry and partly melodrama. The answer was not to punish him but to ignore his tantrums and avoid doing anything sudden that might set him off. Gradually his shows of temperament became less frequent and if he started playing up, the groom would keep working on him regardless. Getting no response, he would soon settle down again.

John and Clare believe in looking after horses as naturally as possible. The horses are regarded as having feelings and individual personalities – like humans. John has a way with horses: it is a gift which makes their attitudes change in his hands. If one of the girls is having difficulty, say with clipping a horse's head, John will take over and the horse will just stand there. It is a gift which earns respect among his staff as well as being an ingredient in his success story.

PART II: A DAY IN THE LIFE

The glow of relaxation that comes over most people at home is intensified for John Whitaker because he spends so much of his time away. Home means a revitalising change from the gypsy-style existence of the show circuit, where he lives out of a horsebox-cum-caravan. When he arrives back at his remote Yorkshire farm nature pulls up the drawbridge against unwanted visits. Scattered neighbours take a friendly interest in the local hero's progress without invading his privacy. The stable yard has an informal air, each person plays his or her well-rehearsed role without waiting for prompting orders from the boss. But the hilltop isolation cannot deter telephoned intrusions and, in the few days before the next departure, there is just so much to do.

When the alarm goes at about 8 a.m., John, who is a sound sleeper, takes a long time to come to. Clare is up and busy straightaway and half an hour later the family gathers in the kitchen for breakfast. John potters around, making toast, pondering how to condense all that needs doing into the day. If he sits down for a minute to catch up with news from the outside world in yesterday's *Yorkshire Post*, Louise or Robert will soon start clambering over him.

Outside in the stable yard the girl grooms have already been at work for an hour, feeding and mucking out about fifteen horses. Their sweaty, back-bending labour is made easier by the deep litter bedding system, which means only the surface muck is removed and a clean layer of shavings sprinkled in its place. They sweep the loose shavings and wisps of hay from the concrete, the dust rising before the broom, everything spotless in their wake. They have worked up quite an appetite by the time they adjourn for breakfast in the caravan.

The deputy jockey, Alan Fazakerley, emerges from another caravan in well-worn work clothes, ready for a morning in the saddle. He is joined by a local lad called John Womersley, who arrives on a motor cycle. He left school with his heart set on a career with horses. Naturally he jumped at the chance to help out at the Whitaker stable in return for lessons; he receives no pay. Alan, young John and the girls tack up the first wave of horses for exercise. Each animal wears boots or bandages to protect his forelegs and his feet are picked out to prevent shavings scattering over the clean yard. The riders then set off for an hour's hacking along stone-walled lanes and tracks with panoramic views and a cool breeze off the Pennines.

John's first ride of the day is the big, good-natured chestnut, Saint Mungo, who will have a schooling session in the small sand arena next to the yard. John selects a snaffle bridle for Mungo, but today decides to leave off both martingale and draw reins, even though the horse sometimes throws up his head. John wants to see how

Mungo is going without artificial aids. He greets the horse with a quiet word and friendly pat, slips off his night rugs and pulls a few wisps of hay from his mane.

In the arena John has competition for the confined space from a cheeky Welsh Mountain pony, his daughter's schoolmaster. It has taken advantage of a broken rail to invade the schooling area to talk to a brood mare in a neighbouring paddock. The arena only measures about 20 yards by 35 yards and the working area is further curtailed by farm equipment in one corner and a barrel and poles in the middle. John, in faded corduroys and cracked leather ankle boots, works round all this without batting an eyelid. After all, it is not unlike the organized chaos of many a show collecting ring.

He spends the first ten minutes at walk and trot, suppling Mungo with circles, U-turns and serpentines. His hands are low and steady, either side of the horse's withers, gently giving and taking the reins in time with the strides. His legs rhythmically nudge the horse's sides, encouraging the horse fully to use his powerful hindquarters. Mungo's head comes down and in, his neck is gently arched and he relaxes his back. The overall shape is rounded and supple, so that the horse is poised to carry out instructions.

One set of instructions involves putting 'bounce' into Mungo's stride. To do this John increases the pressure with his legs, making Mungo's hindquarters work harder to produce more energy. But John does not want that extra effort to go into longer, flatter strides – as it would if he were galloping a racehorse. He wants short, light and springy strides. To achieve this he tactfully restrains Mungo by squeezing the reins in time with the strides, directing the energy upwards.

A second set of instructions covers turns, circles and sideways movements. This means that John's hand and leg aids are telling Mungo which way to go, as well as the speed required; the horse must be able to move away from the rider's leg without accelerating. To teach the horse this subtle obedience, John does a variety of exercises with the horse's body at an angle to the track. With a nudge of the heel, he moves Mungo's hindquarters in towards the centre of the school or out towards the fence. Once the horse has learnt this lesson it will be easier for John to stop him either cutting corners or drifting wide round a turn.

This work lays a sound foundation for the show jumper's most important pace, the canter. This is how John describes it: 'All a show jumper needs to do is lengthen and shorten his canter, make flying changes of leg and maintain balance. The other fancy moves are just to keep him supple and obedient.'

Lengthening and shortening is vital because a horse's normal cantering stride is about 4 yards long, but the margin for error in picking the take-off spot at a 5-foot obstacle is less than 1 yard – the ideal zone is a matter of inches. The last few strides should be even and their gathering power uninterrupted. Adjustments can be made by lengthening or shortening the stride during approach. Longer strides are achieved by the rider urging the horse forward with his legs and seat and giving with his hands. To shorten, the rider resists the forward movement with his hands and back, but he must keep his leg on as well to prevent loss of momentum.

The second requirement is the flying change, which is recognized as a fairly advanced movement in dressage. When cantering on a circle, the inside foreleg should appear to lead the stride, the other legs follow in a set sequence. If the direction is changed the sequence must change and the best point for this to happen is in mid-air, between strides – the so-called flying change. It avoids the need to break down to trot in order to restart the canter on the other leg. John teaches Mungo the flying change over a pole, applying the aids during the small jump. It is important that the fore- and hindlegs change sequence together, otherwise the canter becomes disunited and uncomfortable.

As for the third ingredient, balance, it enables the horse to carry itself and the rider effortlessly through every manoeuvre. It develops with practice, both during schooling sessions and in the show ring. But John believes the aptitude is inborn and it is a natural ability he looks for in the rawest novice.

As if to illustrate what he is aiming for, John tacks up his old favourite, Ryan's Son, and takes him on to the sand for a rare schooling session. He is so experienced and has such a demanding competition programme that his work at home is usually limited to roadwork to keep him fit. However, it is difficult to tell how fit Ryan is. He can be sluggish hacking round the lanes and then act 'like a lunatic' at a show. So the occasional disciplined run through a set of schooling exercises helps to concentrate his mind.

Ryan belies his sixteen years – ten of them on the show jumping circuit. His forelegs are clear of the boney lumps and puffy patches that so often appear under the pressure of a thousand landings a year. On his nearside hindleg you can see the tiny lump, called a curb, which put Andrew Fielder off buying him. It has never affected his performance. He is a tough horse, but credit for his soundness also goes to John for never overjumping him and always using bandages or leather boots to protect those priceless front legs.

Once in the school he does all the suppling exercises with the litheness of a lizard. His understanding of John's imperceptible signals borders on the telepathic, although he sometimes anticipates aids to stop or turn. This is a common fault in intelligent old campaigners, but it can catch the rider with an embarrassing jolt.

At all paces he picks up his hind feet like a dancer and his cantering strides are so active each one has a skip to it. But the crafty so and so occasionally gets bored and throws a string of bucks, destroying rhythm, disuniting his canter and finally breaking down into trot. John smiles indulgently, scolds him like a naughty child and patiently starts again.

Patience and calm are the hallmarks of John's approach to training. He works each horse for about half an hour, without a whip and without punishing it in anger with either his heels or hands. If a horse repeatedly gets a movement wrong, John will firmly tell it 'No' with a nudge of

his legs and a pull on the reins. Then he works to improve
the horse by repeating the exercise and adding variations to
enhance the lesson, gradually persuading him to do exactly
what is required. After a schooling session John takes the
horse for a stroll up the lane to cool off and relax before
returning to the stable, where he gets a final pat and word
of encouragement.

For the next schooling session John moves into the
jumping paddock, which is about 100 yards from the stables.
This time John stays on the ground as trainer, and Alan
Fazakerley and John Womersley do the riding. They are
already warming up their mounts at trot and canter, circ-
ling round the obstacles and frequently changing direction.
Their riding style is less subtle than John's and they employ
a narrower range of exercises. However, they are aiming
for the same response from the horse: a bouncy, balanced
canter and obedience to hand and leg.

John's set of practice fences is no glossy replica of a
show ring course; it is the battered remnants of equipment
collected over many years. The materials are an odd assortment of paint-flaked poles, wings of differing designs and
wooden stands attached to old oil drums. These are
arranged into a single upright and a double, with an
upright as the first part and a spread on the way out. There
is also a wall in wooden sections and a blue board not much
larger than a door – that is the 'water' jump!

A horse and two ponies have free run of the jumping
paddock and neighbouring field for grazing. Fortunately
they are not interested in today's jumping lesson and keep
away from the working horses. But the small, grey-haired
terrier, Mindy, has other ideas. She enjoys chasing the
horses' heels and barking frantically between rolling over
to appeal for fuss. As in the schooling area, all interruptions
are taken in both horse's and rider's stride. It is useful for
a show jumper to develop a police horse-style temperament
to help him cope with the excitement of a busy showground.

John the trainer concentrates on the way each horse is
going, altering the obstacles so that progress is made on
every jump. The ultimate goal is to finish the jumping

session with a clean leap in classic style over a testing fence – bearing in mind the horse's experience. John does not correct the rider's position in the saddle, but he does advise him how to use his hands or legs to get better results from the horse. He also suggests improvements in technique on the approach to an obstacle.

The first to come under the trainer's eye is the teenager, John Womersley, on a common-looking horse called Roman Warrior. 'Handsome is as handsome does' in show jumping and this strongly built, dark bay has a big jump. John starts the session with four trotting poles, laid on the ground about 4 feet apart. This gentle introduction to obstacles encourages a calm approach and improves concentration, a quality which Warrior lacks. John then builds a small fence, with a take-off pole about 9 feet in front of it to guide Warrior's final stride. John likes to use poles on the ground and small fences, jumped from a trot, to improve the horse's attitude. The animal has to think about where to put his feet and rhythm is established. The rider can leave the horse to sort out the obstacle for himself, whereas over a bigger fence he would have to help.

Once the horse has settled, John moves on to the conventional upright and double. Warrior is still an inexperienced horse and John's instructions to the young rider are designed to counteract deviations in the horse's approach. Early on Warrior spooks at a fence and John tells the rider to use his legs to keep the horse straight and prevent hesitation. Later Warrior gets more confident and approaches a fence too fast, knocking it down. John points out that the rider no longer needs to use his legs so strongly. He is as patient with the rider as he is with the horse; both are only making mistakes through inexperience.

It is Alan Fazakerley's turn next on one of the Grade As. Alan has four years' more experience than his young colleague, so John expects more accuracy from him at each fence. After a warm-up over small fences, John concentrates the training session on the double. The first part, an upright, has little filling, making it look flimsy, and the ground in front of it slopes slightly downhill. This makes it a good test of how careful a horse is and how well balanced. The second part is a spread, one stride after the first part. The horse must retain its power in the middle of the double so that it can stretch out over the parallel bars on the way out.

John points out an extra complication to Alan: the distance between the two parts of the double is only 7 yards instead of the usual 8 yards. He says the horse must take off fairly close to the first part, so that he does not jump in too far. If he did fly in with a long, flat jump, he would be too close to the second part and probably knock it down.

Alan tries so hard to obey that he makes his mount stamp in a very short last stride before take-off. This creates extra effort, the horse having to jump nearly vertically to clear the fences. John explains that he wants a happy medium, with the take-off neither too close nor too far from the first fence. He also advises Alan to adjust the stride further from the jump. Seeing a good stride to a fence is a prime skill in show jumping. John can organize the horse's approach about six strides out. The more strides the rider sees before a fence, the better. The next time Alan turns to the double he straightaway shortens the horse for a couple of strides and then lets him go on for three even strides, taking off at the ideal spot. He earns immediate praise from John.

The air of informality surrounding all the activity borders on the absurd when Alan decides to try a newly broken youngster in the schooling area, its companions from the field in tow. The two tiny greys, a Welsh Mountain and a Shetland, don't want to miss the fun when Alan tries their green friend over a few poles. He walks round the track and the other two fit in in front and behind, like a circus act. John stands in the middle enjoying the spectacle. Then he hits on an idea to encourage the youngster to pop over its first jump. It is especially friendly with the Shetland and that could give a lead. John picks up a long slat of wood to drive the Shetland over an 18-inches high pole. It neatly tucks its feet into its belly to clear it, but the gawky youngster, sixty per cent taller than its 10 h.h. mate, blunders through. John will have to wait and see whether it has a latent spring.

The novice has a running martingale on to act as a check if it throws its head up. More experienced animals are often schooled in draw reins. These run from the girth through the snaffle ring to the rider's hands, bringing the horse's head down and in. John has mixed feelings about their value. On the plus side they make life easier for the rider, especially on a strong horse or an older one with bad habits, because both types tend to resist the rider's efforts to put them into the right 'rounded' shape. By helping the rider achieve an obedient response more quickly, the reins save the horse's legs from the strain of extra hours of schooling.

John points out that they should be used with normal reins, so that they do not continue to pressurize the horse when it has brought its head into the right position. If this happens, the horse may start to lean on the reins, which would ultimately harden its mouth and make it heavy in front. John does not school in draw reins every day because there is no benefit if the horse's head goes straight up after the reins come off. Horses which are thoroughly schooled from the beginning, as Novilheiro was for dressage, usually do not need draw reins because they are in the habit of always going in the right shape and their muscles have developed accordingly.

Many child show jumpers copy their heroes by using draw reins all the time on their ponies. John is not keen on this trend because he says youngsters ride mostly with their hands. This means that, with the draw reins on, the danger is that they will continually fight the pony's mouth and spoil it. They don't realize how much leg and seat the top riders use to get their results.

By one o'clock between twelve and sixteen horses have been exercised, the ones which were not due for schooling having had an hour's roadwork. Alan dishes out feeds for the horses before the humans descend on the farmhouse kitchen for a snack lunch. John now has to think about all the considerations other than riding which go with running a busy show jumping yard. Clare has collected various phone messages during the morning – someone wants John to have a ride on his horse to see if it is any good . . . an owner wants to know if his horse is going to a particular show . . . Fred Bloggs has some good hay at £2 a bale.

Clare's day combines the elements of housewife and mother, stable supervisor and administrator. Her time can be consumed clipping a horse, shopping, cooking or totting up a horse's winnings in between sending Louise off to play and changing Robert's nappies. If a foreign show is coming up, she confirms with the British Show Jumping Association which horses John will take and makes sure their papers, including vaccination certificates, are in order. She has no help in the house and has a practical approach to things domestic. After all, housework is not such a tall order for one who has cared for four horses in the past. She would not want John to do the domestic chores, partly for traditional reasons – and partly because it is too late to make him as efficient as she is in the house!

John's afternoon may be spent collecting fodder or seeing a horse. If he stays at home, there is the garden to weed, fences to maintain and the horsebox to restock for the next show tour. There are not many odd jobs to which he has not turned his hand, from fixing the television in the horsebox to demolishing old hen houses.

Clare usually prepares the evening meal, although John can cook if he must. He helps out with the children, including the nappy changing and bathing. He has plenty of patience with Louise and Robert – as he has with the horses – and can turn a fractious child into a compliant one. His placid nature means he can keep his temper with them when others would be tearing their hair. Clare reckons he would have half a dozen children given half a chance.

After dinner she settles down at her desk to fill in entry forms. John and Alan go to two or three shows a week; most last between one and three days and some have show jumping classes in two or three rings. Classes are carefully picked for each individual horse according to his grade, experience and temperament. A bold horse new to Grade A will be prepared to tackle a major competition over 5-foot fences sooner than one that will refuse if in doubt about his ability to clear a jump. Clare and John discuss each horse's programme as she fills in the forms.

The Whitakers enjoy staying in during the evening because they spend so much time away. Their social life, as well as John's career, revolves around the caravans and temporary stables of Britain's agricultural shows and specialist show jumping venues. Even a comparatively quiet evening at home will see decisions made about the horses, phone calls made and received and the children given attention. John and Clare rarely get to bed before midnight.

After a particularly hard day, John will doze off in front of the television. He is one of those people who can sleep anywhere, anytime, a quality of immense importance when rest has to be squeezed between driving a lorry up and down the country and long days at home or at shows, where life is just as hectic.

6

Off to the Shows

PART I: PREPARATION

John and Clare spend so much time going away to shows
that their live-in horsebox, part of a travelling show
jumping village, has become a home from home. For the
girl grooms, too, preparing horses for the show ring is as
well practised a routine as the more conventional pattern
of work at home. For all of them, including the children,
going to shows means meeting friends and keeping up with
the sport's news and gossip, as well as being a public test
of horse and rider.

Before a show the competing horses have their manes
and tails shampooed. Soap is not used on their bodies as it
would remove too much natural oil; instead the girls rely
on daily elbow grease to keep the coats clean and glossy.
They run through a grooming sequence that would exhaust
a beginner, first raising the dirt from the hair roots with a
rubber curry comb, then whisking off the bits with a dandy
brush. The polishing phase starts with the softer, short-
bristled body brush, which removes the fine dust. The mass-
aging motion also stimulates oil production in the skin,
giving the coat its gloss. A wipe over with a cloth produces
the ultimate shine. At the show dark brown hoof oil will
be painted on to add the finishing touch. Similar care goes
into tack cleaning. The girls use a damp sponge to remove
the dirt and then rub in saddle soap to feed the leather,
making it supple and gleaming. Metalwork is polished,
except for the bits. Both horses and tack get this scrupulous

treatment every day so there is no build-up of dirt to add work to an already crammed timetable.

On the morning of the show the girls start work earlier than usual because coiffuring the performers has to be added to the usual routine of feeding, mucking out, grooming and exercising. They put about twelve plaits in each mane, using rubber bands to secure them in neat balls. This dextrous job only takes the experienced groom a quarter of an hour. The stallion, Novilheiro, has his silky grey mane combed but left loose, as is the tradition with Andalusian horses.

Loading equipment into the horsebox is quite a marathon, especially if the team is staying away for two or three weeks. For the horse the saddle and bridle is only a start. He also needs boots to protect his legs from knocks: the tendons and heels at the back of the forelegs are particularly vulnerable. To stop him slipping a variety of studs is available, the shape and size used depending on the state of the going. Two will be screwed into each shoe just before the class. It is one of the more back-breaking chores. For schooling, draw reins are packed with a couple of old bridles to save dirtying the show set. Even in the warmest weather the horses will wear lightweight rugs in the stable, as much to keep their coats smooth and clean as to protect against draughts. So that sweat can dry quickly there is a special rug which looks like a string vest. Overnight stays mean the fodder bins which line one side of the horsebox must be replenished; bales of hay are stowed on a rack at the back of the lorry and water buckets and lightweight feed troughs are stacked. Grooming kit and tack and boot cleaning gear complete the list of basics.

For the show ring John needs to pack his velvet-covered hard hat, red jacket for the grand arena, tweed one for the minor classes, white ties, jodhpurs and boots. To keep these spotless he will change into them at the last minute. Extras include riding sticks and pairs of spurs – John will change from one set to another, or leave them off altogether, depending which horse he is riding. Clare is in charge of stocking up the living quarters at the front of the box. The fridge and larder cupboard are filled, clothes folded away in drawers and suitcases and the baby's cot and pushchair put on board. Toys and books are taken along to amuse the children and, if Louise is lucky, there may be space to ferry her Shetland pony to the show. That keeps her enthralled for longer than all the other gear put together.

With so many things to remember, it is not surprising that occasionally something important gets left behind. One year they arrived at the Royal Highland, near Edinburgh, to find none of the saddles had been put on board. One of the grooms was very red-faced about the omission. Friends were on hand to lend saddles for the first day and luckily Mr Brown was travelling up from West Yorkshire and could bring John's set. Every rider prefers a saddle he is used to and which has brought him luck in the past.

One thing which cannot be forgotten is the kit that the horses travel in to protect them from draughts, knocks or scuffs of their neatly pulled tails. They wear warm rugs, thick leg bandages rolled on over gamgee tissue and an elasticated tail bandage. In the horsebox each has an individual stall and stands on anti-slip rubber mats, which can be easily removed and cleaned. If the team travels on the same day as the competitions, it is essential to reach the show ground at least an hour before John's first event in order to declare his intention to jump and make any substitutions of horses for the ones originally entered.

One day the procedure went completely awry when the Whitaker entourage turned up for a show on the wrong date. It was an indoor event at Stoneleigh, Warwickshire, on the Royal Show site. John rolled the lorry up to park near the school and at first was impressed that they were for once the first to arrive. But, when they peered into the arena and saw no jumps and no people, the penny dropped. They had got the day of the week right, but the show was not until seven days later. They just had to turn round and trek 130 miles home.

John does virtually all the horsebox driving, having passed his Heavy Goods Vehicle test as soon as he reached twenty-one. The hours on the road between riding at shows and arriving at the next destination can be mindboggling. The longest haul John has done in Britain was going straight up to the Royal Highland after competing on the last day of the Cardiff Castle show. The journey took about eight hours and John only had time to snatch a few hours sleep before getting ready for his first class in Scotland. Late night driving is commonplace for him as his team prefers to leave a show straight after the last class, even if it is 11 p.m. He keeps himself awake with coffee, cigarettes and the radio.

Whenever possible they travel to more distant shows the day before, giving both humans and horses a chance to get installed at the show site and to have a proper rest before competing. The Whitakers share this process with their friends as the show jumping village pitches camp by rows of temporary stables and – if they are lucky – camp-site facilities.

From the outside the horseboxes look like mobile bill boards, advertising the companies sponsoring the competitors. John's horsebox and that of his brother, Michael, have the grey and burgundy livery of the Next fashion shops. Inside, the lorries serve as home, tack room and feed store. John, Clare and the children live in caravan-style quarters at the front of the box. On one side is the kitchen and on the other the dining room-cum-bedroom. There is extra sleeping space in the luton over the cab. The groom sleeps in the back of the lorry, the mats the horses travelled on are pulled up and the wooden floor scrupulously swept. Clothes and tack hang side by side along the walls.

Between the horseboxes are an assortment of caravans, cars and motorbikes. The casually dressed population could belong to any camp site. Sticky-fingered children run around in various stages of undress and terriers rifle the rubbish sacks. You can only pick out the riders when they emerge in brilliant white breeches, black boots and red coats. For brief trips to the ringside they squat astride mini-motorcycles, a parody of their usual mounts.

John always tries to park the horsebox as near as possible to the stables to cut down the time and effort of carting haynets, feeds and tack. The disadvantage is that some hungry horse will start banging for its breakfast at dawn! Between the rows, sawdust from the horses' bedding mingles with the summer dust that wears through flattened grass. Around the water taps the slops from hundreds of buckets create a slippery mud patch. During the day you can see blue-jeaned girls – and a few lads – busy brushing horses tied outside the stables, or standing on stools to plait manes. After tea there is a rush to the showers, followed by a bee-line to the nearest bar. Late at night many of the grooms will slip back to the stables to put an additional rug on their charges and top up water buckets.

However late the night, there is no chance of a lie-in the next day, with three or four horses to prepare for competition. As well as the usual stable chores, there are horses to exercise while the schooling area is comparatively quiet. John often likes to put the horse he will jump in the big class through its paces in the morning. In this way he can curb any over-exuberance and restore concentration, so that when he comes to warm up twenty minutes before the real thing the horse will get straight down to work.

The riders' first sight of the course is on foot and this is when the crowd has its first look at them. They inspect the numbered fences, memorising the route. They check the height, width and solidity of the obstacles, gauge the turns, so that each approach will be straight, and pace distances between related fences. This last job is particularly important and explains why John and his colleagues take deliberate yard-long steps between fences which are close together. The number of yards tells him how many strides his horse should take. Since a good distance will allow 4 yards for every cantering stride plus a total of 4 yards for take-off and landing, 20 yards should allow a comfortable four strides.

But the distance may not be exact – probably a deliberate move by the course builder to test riding skill. If it is longer than the norm, the rider will have to push on for longer strides to reach the right take-off point. If it is shorter, he will have to check for shorter ones. In between, for example

22 yards, he has to decide between four or five strides. John explains, 'If you choose four long ones you have to make arrangements before you jump the first so that you can push on when you land.'

With Ryan's Son John generally goes for shorter, bouncy strides, although Ryan is amenable to both ways of riding. One of his good points is that he can shorten and lengthen easily. John usually does not fix a plan for distances above 22 yards, because he will have enough strides to play with as he lands over the first fence in a line. Combinations demand particular accuracy; about 8 yards between parts is one stride, a dozen, two. The approach is all important: 'If it is short and you come in too fast, it is impossible to clear the second part and the problem gets worse through the combination.'

Once he has walked the course John will have decided whether it suits the horse he had intended to jump. With Ryan it does not matter how big the fences are because John knows he can cope with them. It can even be an advantage if the course is stiff because he then regards it as more of a challenge and knows there will be fewer clears to race against the clock.

He always sticks to the adage 'horses for courses' and decides against jumping if the course is not right for the horse he has available. When he started Novilheiro at shows in 1984 he took him to the Royal Cornwall for his first serious classes. The horse apparently responded well, winning a second prize. But John could feel he was putting everything into it; he was overjumping and John sensed he was a bit frightened. The next day he walked the course for the main class and found it was a bit bigger than the day before. He did not want to scare Novilheiro and decided to jump him in a smaller competition instead.

John's approach is more subtle than just avoiding over-facing a horse. Novilheiro is capable of jumping a big course, but if he does so time after time, it would take too much out of him and he would not last so long as a winner. John stresses that a horse must be confident and should ideally be kept to courses which he can do comfortably.

57

He acknowledges that this is far easier for a rider with a string of top-class horses. He remembers when he did not have the luxury of his present choice and the same applied to his brother, Michael, as he tried to break into the top flight. Michael was ambitious and had secured his first decent ride, Brother Scot. But the little horse had to put everything into the major classes as those were the ones Michael needed to go in to get noticed. Brother Scot won for a while, but it did not last. He lost his nerve and would panic in mid-air, paddling between the poles.

To prepare his horse for jumping, John will loosen him up at walk and trot. Work starts in earnest at the canter. John runs through a variety of exercises in the collecting ring to ensure his mount is responsive on circles in both directions, and willing to lengthen or shorten his stride on command. To make sure he is concentrating and obedient, John occasionally halts and reins back for a few paces. This also encourages the horse to bring his hindlegs underneath him, which adds to the spring in his stride.

When John feels his horse is thoroughly worked in at canter, he turns his attention to the practice jumps. Most collecting rings have an upright and a spread, although if space is limited, picking your chance to go can be like negotiating Hyde Park Corner. John introduces the horse over a small upright. As the top pole is raised he wants to feel him snapping off the ground with his front end and neatly tucking away his forelegs. Over the spread John wants to maintain the carefulness but also feel the horse stretching out. If Ryan is feeling cheeky he can exaggerate the swing of his hindquarters into a kick back. After negotiating both upright and spread in classic style, horse and rider are ready to go.

PART II: IN THE RING

No matter how slick the preparation, the crunch comes when the rider enters the ring. Although John is still in the younger generation of top riders, twenty years of show experience is more than enough to tell him that sometimes rounds will go exactly according to plan – but at other times there will be silly mistakes and disasters. His chance to compete at the Montreal Olympics was ruined by a string of stops in just one round at Hickstead. In 1983 he watched his friend, Nick Skelton, have his European Championship hopes dashed by a fall at the Royal International Horse Show.

Of course, most unfortunate rounds are far less drastic in their effects on the future. But they are always bad enough to throw away all chance of winning a prize. Here are a couple of examples and most weeks on the show circuit will throw up similar tales.

One of John's favourite shows is the Great Yorkshire, near Harrogate. As a native of the county he takes special pride in winning there, and every time he dismounts after collecting a rosette a crowd of young fans, even larger than usual, will descend on the local hero. The programme in 1983 included a speed class, with the rich reward of a £900 first prize, and it attracted more than fifty runners.

John jumped early on Charlie's Angel. It was her first competition after a rest and John did not rush her. He knew her clear would only be fast enough for a minor place. His greater expectations rested on Novilheiro, who was winning nearly every time out. The commentator duly informed the partisan Yorkshire crowd of the stallion's triumphs. The build-up, dwelling on Novilheiro's prowess against the clock, went on until John was about to pass through the start.

The crowd was expecting a searing clear. Their anticipation lasted about five seconds. After a tight turn to the second fence, a small upright into a double, Novilheiro refused. A great moan went up from the crowd and the fact that John continued without mistake only added to the anti-climax. It was left to fellow Yorkshireman Harvey Smith to give the spectators the local win they wanted. Novilheiro's misdemeanor was a reminder that horses have minds of their own and are not machines. They are the best things for bringing down to earth anyone who gets complacent.

Sometimes their rejection of a rider's orders is understandable. At the 1983 Horse of the Year Show at Wembley John jumped Charlie's Angel in the puissance competition, famous for its big red wall. Although stockily built and standing less than 16 h.h., the bustling grey mare had three times jumped more than 7 feet. At 6 feet 10 inches, the wall was already 19 inches higher than her and she could not be seen from the other side as John rode down to it. She cleared it and went into the final three-horse jump off to face the wall at 7 feet 1½ inches.

As John urged her on through the final energy-gathering strides before take-off he was sure she was going to jump it. But at the last moment she dug in her heels and John sailed over her shoulder. He dismissed the fall afterwards with a smile, saying it was 'in slow motion'. He had the consolation of a £1,300 prize through sharing second place with Lionel Dunning; only the winner, Eddie Macken on Carroll's Royal Lion, cleared the wall.

Charlie did not forget the unpleasant experience, even though her next competition was a speed class over much smaller fences. The third fence was a wall and she stopped at it. John did not punish her, although she should have jumped it. He understood her reluctance after the puissance and also he did not carry a stick when jumping her indoors. He said she was so strong he could not manage one as well as the reins when she was pulling! He knew that she thought she had got away with defiance. Next time he would try not to give her a chance to stop and, if she did, she would have to have a smack. 'You have to let them know that they are not going to get away with it. They are like children; if they think they can get away with something, they try it on', he said.

Fortunately for John there are far more classes where things go just right. And there was a good example at the same Horse of the Year Show in the first big class, the £2,000-to-the-winner Canon Camera Stakes.

John and Ryan's Son were among twelve clear rounds

going into the jump-off against the clock. They were fifth to go and had the speed merchants, Harvey Smith, Nick Skelton and Geoff Glazzard, behind them. John knew he could cut the corners as finely as anyone. He can tell Ryan before take-off which way to go on landing by combining the signals to go left or right with those for the jump. But the other ingredients of a fast round, cutting down the number of strides between fences and pushing on for speed, used not to suit Ryan. It would make his strides too long and flat and so interfere with his usual careful jumping.

Surprisingly, at the age of fifteen, Ryan was still improving! John went into the jump-off prepared to take an extra risk right at the start of the course. Lesley McNaught had already done a fast time, so there was no point in hanging around. John set sail through the start, flew the first fence and immediately pushed Ryan on to take four strides instead of five to the second. Such was his control of the horse that he could still check immediately on landing and turn back tightly for the third. The round continued in this daring fashion and he set a target which completely foiled the opposition. They either made mistakes trying to catch him, or took care to clear the fences and clocked slow times.

It was nice for John to know that Ryan was going as well – or even better – than ever. But as his old favourite had won virtually every major competition, there were other victories which give him even more pleasure. One of these was at Hickstead during the 1983 Derby meeting.

The day before the Derby, John took Ryan and Saint Mungo in the big class. With Ryan, his thoughts were on the Derby. He took him round for a school and this relaxed approach to a tough course left two fences down. For Saint Mungo the class was a milestone; he had rarely jumped at Hickstead and his programme was generally county shows, not full-blown internationals. He was hardly noticed in the press box – until he jumped a clear round, one of only three in the competition. Then the questions started buzzing . . . What is this horse? How old is he? How long has John been riding him . . .?

John was first to go in the jump-off and behind him were two senior international riders on experienced horses, David Broome on Queensway Royale and Derek Ricketts on Money Market. Mungo has a long stride and had competed in speed classes in the huge arena; he felt confident, so John decided to have a go. He set a scorching pace and Mungo made nothing of the fences. David Broome had 4 faults and was 4 seconds slower. Derek Ricketts cut the corners and stayed clear, but still failed to catch Mungo's time.

When John rang Mungo's owner, Mr Fred Brown, that evening to tell him of the victory, Mr Brown said he had rarely heard him so excited. John was delighted that the nine-year-old had made the grade in such a positive way and that his view that Mungo had Olympic potential was confirmed.

It is just that sort of challenge, to guide a young horse to its first big win and make the sport's officials sit up and take note, that really gets John's adrenalin going. And that is when he is at his best. His father-in-law, Malcolm Barr, sometimes jokes that if he could think of a way to goad John before a big competition he would, to rouse his fighting spirit.

One of John's best friends on the circuit, Nick Skelton, says that although John never looks to get excited, when he is determined 'he breathes fire'. That is the other side to a personality which is apparently quiet and unassuming and never gets het up. It would be wrong to think that his placid nature means he is soft. Nick's verdict is that he is as tough as anyone when he gets his back up, and that includes being firm with a naughty horse. It is a sign that he cares deeply about his performance and is too proud to allow a let down to pass without action.

Nick acknowledges John as one of the best riders in the world. However, he reckons most people will never realize how good he is because of his quiet style. His record has two outstanding features: his great achievement with Ryan and his numerous wins on all sorts of other horses. With Ryan he had won more than £200,000 by the end of 1984 and was on his way to setting a record Nick felt would be impossible to beat. Another mark of the pair's consistency was that John never rode any other horse in Nations Cups before 1984, nine years after he first jumped for Britain on Ryan.

However, John also wins frequently on different types of horse, as is shown by his consistently high position in the riders' computer rankings, which tots up winnings on all Grade A horses. Nick points out that John is fast against the clock on all his rides and always a worry if he is behind him in a jump-off.

There is a fun side to show jumping, however, which does occasionally come under the spotlight. One of the best examples is the fancy dress pairs competition at the Christmas Olympia Show. John and Nick have made quite a name for themselves in this competition. But some of John's earlier efforts with other riders also brought the house down. He played an authentic-looking Kermit to Tony Newbery's Miss Piggy when the Muppets were all the rage. Another of his bright ideas was to 'dress up' as a streaker.

Just as John is not so placid as he looks in the ring, he can also let his hair down on a night out, with a gallon of beer inside him. Or as Fred Brown once put it, 'He can be quite mischievous when he's out with the lads.'

Nick recalls one night in Bordeaux, France, when he, John and the Australian rider, Kevin Bacon, returned to the hotel after a few drinks. Eddie Macken should have gone out with them, but had felt unwell and stayed in his room, which was next to John's on the third storey.

Nick went into Kevin's room for a drink. Then they suddenly realized John had disappeared. They started to search for him and found the clothes he had been wearing discarded on his bed. His jeans were missing. They looked everywhere for him, ending up back in John's room.

Looking out of the window, they saw John lying on his back on the ground in the middle of some bushes. Tell-tale scrapes on the wall showed where he had slipped down, scrabbling with his feet and fingers. Their fears were allayed when they noticed he had a lit cigarette and appeared to be in no pain. Kevin went down, picked him up and led him back to his room. John's explanation was that he had been trying to climb over to Eddie's room as a 'surprise.' No sooner had the trio settled down for another drink than John was out of the window again for another go. He found exactly the same route down the wall into the bushes and lit up another cigarette to contemplate the problem as he lay on his back.

His satirical wit can cut through the most sober circumstances – even at the Substitute Olympics at Rotterdam. Nick was watching a class with Graham Fletcher and one obstacle had caught everyone's eye. It was a huge bank with a table top and in the middle of the plateau was a big ditch with a jump over it. But because the top was lined with fir trees, all you could see was the horses going on and coming off.

When John's turn came, his round was uneventful until he disappeared behind the fir trees. An almighty crash sounded from the top of the bank. Nick and Graham conjured up pictures of John and horse lying in the ditch under a pile of broken poles. There was no movement among the firs, not a sound. They rushed into the ring, fearing the worst, scrambled up the side of the bank and pulled aside a bush. There was John, sitting on his horse smiling. He looked at them and said, 'I wondered when you were going to come.'

The unflappable side of John's nature is a great asset on marathon trips abroad when he and Nick often travel together. John never panics, and takes irritations like running out of fuel in his stride. He just gets out of the cab, walks five miles up the road with a can and comes back with it full of diesel. He will also drive all day and all night. The longest non-stop trip John has done was thirty-six hours on a journey back from Poland.

Most of his horses travel well and Ryan even manages to rest, despite the effort of balancing as the lorry turns or brakes. He can go into the box tired and come out fresh after a few hours on the road. Some horses panic and kick at the box, thus endangering themselves; these are a liability which John is glad to avoid. However, even relatively calm travellers can feel queasy, although horses are not physically capable of being sick.

To get back from Spain in May 1984 John's horses were on the road for several days. They were stabled overnight en route, but the unusually long hours on the road, day after day, made Hopscotch travel sick. He refused to eat and started shaking. John and Clare were not with the lorry, but the horses were in good hands and the driver pulled in and parked until the chestnut recovered. It delayed the journey for half a day, but it was a slight inconvenience compared with subjecting the horse to distress.

The most frightening accident John can remember was with his skewbald pony, Crazy Horse. He was lined up in the lorry with about five others. It was a Whitaker family outing and John was with the ponies in the back, which turned out to be the saving grace for Crazy Horse. As the horsebox went round a roundabout John's mother had to stop quickly and all the ponies leant on the one at the front. Crazy Horse's legs went straight through the floor and one of his hooves came to rest on the prop shaft. John leapt out and warned his mother not to move the box. They unloaded the ponies and carefully helped Crazy Horse to extricate himself from the hole. By a miracle he was only grazed, and after a check for injuries and rearrangements in the box to avoid the hole, he walked straight back in.

7

Support

PART I: NURTURING TALENT

The idea of John needing support sounds a bit strange at first to those who know him. Independence and self-sufficiency are strong traits in his character and he is not the sort of person who goes seeking help. However, you do not have to look far into his life to discover that support from his family and other show jumping enthusiasts has run parallel with the development of his innate resources.

The nurturing of his talent started, of course, with his parents. His mother's teaching did not stop once he had grasped the basics. She continued to keep him on the right lines and there was no chance that he would develop bad habits under her eye. Just as important as the mechanics of riding was his parents' approach to horses. Both had generations of family knowledge to draw on through their farming roots. Show jumping was a departure from this tradition, but looking after horses and getting to know how they ticked did not change much. The practical attitude inherited from working with animals gave John a more healthy view of horses than that of sentimental towns-people, who graduate to them from smaller pets.

Once John had decided show jumping was the life for him, his parents gave him every encouragement. Financially they did what they could. When they could afford an animal with promise, like Singing Wind, they bought it, and John learnt much from taking on horses which had yet to reach their potential. To this day he would much rather take his mounts on a rising path to the top than have the responsibility and possibility of failure that goes with sitting on an expensive one, well-established by someone else.

John's parents' farm became adapted for horses, enabling him and Michael – and later Steven – to take in a string of horses for schooling and competition. Enid Whitaker drove the horsebox and acted as groom and groundsman, able to give a different perspective on the way the horse jumped and the way the boys rode. If anything went wrong they would mull it over together, work out the reason and try to find a solution. When other riders made mistakes, their cases would become meat for the process of chewing over how best to achieve clear rounds or be the fastest against the clock.

Moral support was just as important. John's parents' belief in his ability never wavered, and his father in particular would stick up for him – even on his off days. John remembers going with his father to Harewood show, near Leeds, to compete in a £4,000 class. 'I jumped a clear and then took the wrong course in the second round. I was really sick and said to my father I must be going daft. He just replied, "Never mind." He didn't show he was bothered and I started getting a bit mad with him because he was not cross with me. He's the sort of person who, if I got eight out of ten fences down, would say, "you jumped the other two well"!'

However, for all their keenness, John's mother and father never pressurized him. He feels sorry for children pushed too much by their parents, to the extent that it causes upset and arguments. And he was never spoilt. His mother was a stickler for high standards in the stable yard; work was the prime virtue and if something went wrong you looked to put it right next time, rather than feel sorry for yourself. Any sign of decadence, like staying out late, would be literally swept away, as the head of the broom hit his backside.

However, the conscientiousness rubbed off. John is a self-critical rider and does not mind admitting when he is at fault. He will sometimes blame himself when the horse could have tried harder. 'You can usually find a reason for a mistake. Eighty per cent of the time if the rider had done something different, the horse would probably have cleared the fence.' However, once judgment has been passed John is not one to brood.

He does not always escape criticism from his supporters. If he jumps a clear but incurs a time fault, he knows he can expect a bit of a dig: 'Did you stop for a coffee?' is what Mr Barr might say. And John's wife, Clare, will also let him know what she thinks of a below par round.

John reckons it is more nerve-racking to watch than to take part. He has experienced the quickening heartbeat as one of his brothers or a close friend waits at the ring entrance for a crucial round, the churning stomach as they jump each fence and the surge of joy as they successfully clear the last.

When John is in the ring there is nothing Clare can do to help. Outside, when decisions have to be made, she is fiercely protective of his interests. Her opportunities for expressing her views to the sport's powers that be are limited, but she will always point out pitfalls to John and warn him against exploitation. One move that annoyed her was when the selectors put pressure on him to take Ryan's Son to jump in the Nations Cup at Dublin after the horse's exertions in winning two silver medals at the 1983 European Championships. John's inclination, backed by Clare, was to give Ryan an immediate holiday, and take a younger horse. But Ronnie Massarella made a special plea for him to go and he believed fellow championship team member, Malcolm Pyrah, was making a similar concession with Anglezarke.

Malcolm Pyrah managed to evade the request and Britain's weakened Nations Cup team finished last in Dublin. It was a frustrating anticlimax and John knew Ryan had lost his edge. Clare made it clear that he should not have gone and that next time he should stick to his guns. She is more suspicious of people's motives than John and will point out that things are not as straightforward as they seem.

She believes in being discreet about her views: 'I don't

shout about it or run to the papers.' However, she has been
known to take independent action. During the build-up to
the Los Angeles Olympics much manoeuvring went on to
try to fix up shortlisted riders with decent horses. David
Broome and his backer, Phil Harris, received compensation
for lending Mr Ross and Tony Elliott, of Griffin and Brand
European, received a lot of attention as the Griffin and
Brand horses were transferred from Lionel Dunning's yard
to prospective Olympic riders. But the owners, like Mr
Brown, who had made their horses freely available all along
did not even get a thank you, let alone a share of the fuss
the selectors bestowed on the ones that needed wooing.

Clare did not approve and felt particularly disappointed
for the Brown family, who had been so loyal to John. After
the injustice had been discussed for a few weeks she sat
down and wrote a letter to the British Show Jumping
Association, pointing out that owners who had been
generous with their horses all along were just as deserving
of thanks as those making an Olympic run. Mr Brown did
subsequently get a thank you letter.

Apart from being John's alter ego during decision
making, Clare provides a mind-boggling amount of practical support. She knows about all the stages of show
jumping, from grooming to the programme of entries for
each horse. Having competed herself, she also understands
the technicalities. She is super-efficient and in many ways
boss of the yard.

One winter one of the grooms, Mandy Thomas, left for a
few months to try more conventional work in a shop, but
soon tired of it and missed the horses. It was Clare whom
she rang to ask if she could come back, and it was Clare who
decided yes. She also manages the books, keeping records of
the amount of prize money each horse has won, sending
bills to owners and accounting for the continual stream of
cheques to pay the bills of running a fifteen horse competition yard.

The figures Clare deals with run into tens of thousands
of pounds each year. Just keeping the horses is the most
expensive item as the stables are virtually full all year

round. The family owns about half the inmates, including shares in two stallions. Others are sent by owners for either the indoor or the outdoor seasons. And there are often one or two horses spending a few weeks with the Whitakers for schooling and assessment of their talent.

The show jumpers at competition fitness, whether they be grade A or novice, munch their way through three feeds a day on top of nearly half a bale of hay each. Their menu includes horse nuts, oats, bran and sugar beet pulp. In 1985 the cost of fodder alone is more than £20 a week per horse. Other regular bills are for wood-shaving bedding and sets of shoes. Each horse gets a new set every three to four weeks.

John's horsebox clocks up about 15,000 miles a year and is ferried across the Channel and the North and Irish seas. He also makes several flights to shows or to see horses. The second horsebox, carrying Alan's team to national shows, does about 5,000 miles annually. Entering for shows is quite an expense, especially if stabling on the show ground must be hired. Clare fills in the forms several weeks before the event and sends off cheques for up to £300.

Other bills arise from employing four people, who all live in; running two horseboxes and cars; entry fees; equipment; and the overheads of a farmhouse and stable yard. The total comes to roughly £65,000 at 1985 prices. That does not include depreciation; new investment in buildings or horses; supporting two children; buying clothes; household goods; or any comforts for the family. Nor does it include remuneration for Clare, the professional responsible for running the yard, or 'pocket money' for John, the amateur.

The diagram opposite shows approximately where the money goes.

The money to pay for it all comes from owners and from sponsorship by the Next fashion shop company. The British Show Jumping Association pays expenses when John represents his country. Officially, the prize money he wins – about £71,000 in 1984 – goes to the owners, and it is up to them to decide how much to give him. In practice, arrangements between John and the owners are diverse.

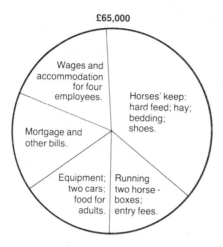

£65,000

Some pay livery fees and show expenses but keep most of the prize money; others divide the prize money with John, giving him a generous share so that expenses are more than covered. If a horse improved by John is sold for a profit, he will also expect commission. Clare plays a major role in these negotiations, both as an astute businesswoman and because she is the professional through whom the money must be channelled to preserve John's amateur status.

However, the origin of each deal is the horse. John acknowledges that it is financially impossible for him and Clare to buy and keep all the horses. They have to rely on other people. It is usually the owners who approach him. Often, like Mr Barr and Mr Brown, they have become involved in show jumping through their children. When circumstances change – perhaps the child gives up or finds one horse unsuitable – the owner decides to pick a new rider. John also gets horses from owner-riders who compete at local shows for fun and then find they have a horse who could go further in expert hands.

When John takes on a horse it is usually either still a novice or yet to reach its potential. At that stage he has the power. He is the one who has been sought out and the owner will be grateful that such a well-known rider has accepted his horse. Once it starts winning, the boot can change to the other foot. As the value of the horse rises the owner may be tempted to sell and make a lot of money. Control always rests ultimately with the owner and he is free to change riders whenever he wishes.

John's experience with owners has generally been happy, partly because he has attracted support from very loyal people and partly through his efforts to give them good value. However, he remembers the occasional hitch with a couple of his early patrons. He had a great deal of success with a horse called Golden Vale, a pale chestnut with a dorsal stripe, whom he rode for the Bericote Stud. This stud was based at riding stables near Stratford-upon-Avon, Warwickshire, and the man behind it was Mr Dennis Rose. But the ambitious plans Mr Rose had for the stud did not carry through, he sold Golden Vale and soon afterwards financial difficulties ended the project.

John was sorry to see Golden Vale go; at that stage in the mid-seventies a good second string to Ryan was hard to find. But he knew Mr Rose had had a good offer and he understood that he needed the money. Nowadays an owner usually seeks John's advice before selling a horse and may allow his view to be the deciding factor. John's attitude is realistic: if the horse has reached its peak, he will generally advise the owner to sell.

Another early experience led John to show a rare flash of temper. He won a couple of classes on the first day of a show with one owner's horse. But the next day he got involved in two jump-offs running simultaneously. The organizers of the more important class would not wait for him to compete in an outer ring, so he missed one jump-off. The owner was very displeased and told John sarcastically, 'You missed the last class, you mustn't bother with the next.'

John explained what had happened and apologized, but the man continued to complain. In the end John told him what he could do with his horses and did not jump any of

hn savours winning the individual silver medal on Ryan's Son in the European ampionships at Hickstead in 1983. With him is Ronnie Massarella

Some of the other horses which have helped John stay at the top, taking the pressure off Ryan's Son

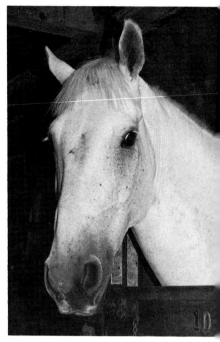

Above: John jumping Saint Mungo, his reserve horse for the Los Angeles Olympics

Right: Charlie's Angel, the Irish-bred grey mare who could jump higher than seven feet, pictured at John's yard in 1983

Left: The indoor specialist, Clonee Temple, a Grand Prix winner on the continent

Below: Hopscotch winning the Foxhunter Championship at the Horse of the Year Show, 1981

Rushgreen at the Royal Show in 1980

The Argentinian-bred thoroughbred, San Salvador, at the City of Leicester Show in 1984

And Novilheiro, the Andalusian stallion who mixes show jumping with serving mares

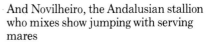

John's back-up rider Alan Fazakerley on Novilheiro in the Whitaker yard

Left: John's first significant backer, later to become his father-in-law, Malcolm Bar~

Below: Michael Whitaker on his Olympic mare Overton Amanda at the Royal Show in 1984

them for a couple of weeks. Then the pair made it up –
after John had received an apology.

Apart from success, an important ingredient in the
owner/rider relationship is communication. John or Clare
will keep the owner informed about the horse's progress,
explain decisions, relive a victory and give reasons for a
mistake. Some owners like to say their piece to John. He
listens – the comments might be helpful – avoids disagree-
ment and carries on doing his own thing.

PART II: JOHN'S BACKERS

For all his independence, John enjoys knowing that others
are behind him. 'They will you on and I get great satisfaction out of telling an owner that his horse has won.' His
enthusiasm reflects one of the best elements of show
jumping: the family-style relationship between a rider and
his long-term supporters.

For Malcolm and Elaine Barr this has, of course, literally
come true through John and Clare's marriage. However,
when Mr Barr first turned to his wife at the Rochdale show
and said of John, 'That boy's the best rider in this class,'
there were still eight years to go before the wedding.

Mr Barr's initial connection with the Whitakers was a
run-of-the-mill arrangement for John to try to make something of his hunter, Rufus the Red. He chose John because
he admired his riding, but there was no question of giving
a Cinderella figure the big break he needed. The link was
businesslike, Mr Barr was sent regular bills for livery fees
and show expenses and he received the prize money. When
the horse had improved substantially he was sold for a good
profit. However, by the time that had happened, Mr and
Mrs Barr were hooked on show jumping and Clare had
fallen for John.

Show jumping has several attractions for the horse
owner. Unlike racing, where the trainer intervenes, there
is a direct and close link with the rider, whom the owner
carefully chooses for personality as well as skill. He then

becomes one of a small circle of backers, all of whom receive personal attention. Unlike a jockey, the show jumper always works the horse at home and rides it at all its shows. There are plenty of opportunities for the owner to watch his horse compete because during the season it has two or three classes a week.

Like all sport, show jumping has a club aspect and lively social life. Owners will find friends and entertainment outside the ring as well as the chance to be associated with success inside it. As clubs go, show jumping is far from exclusive. The people involved are from diverse backgrounds and by no means all wealthy. The sport has drawn in as many business people from towns as country dwellers. Unlike eventing, which has kept a more county air, shows often have an urban setting. The absence of royalty, and the presence of earthy souls like Harvey Smith, have preserved it from an upper class image. Listen to any group of show jumpers talk and accents will have more to do with region than class.

Owners are well and truly involved in the sport. They mingle with riders in the collecting ring, join them in the horsebox kitchen for coffee and a chat and go out for meals with them. They will often look after the horses at their homes in the close season or even between each series of shows. Mr Barr used to enjoy galloping Ryan about the wintry North Yorkshire countryside to get him fit for the spring shows. Mr Brown can see his horses grazing from his living room and admire their handsome heads looking over stable doors opposite the kitchen. Both men have also become involved in the British Show Jumping Association. Mr Barr is on the executive committee and chairs the finance committee, Mr Brown is a regional representative of BSJA members. However, it is the family aspect which exerts the deepest pull.

Mr Brown has an agricultural and construction equipment business at Otley and also farms on the panoramic heights between the River Wharfe and its tributary, the Washburn. He describes his interest in horses as being visited on him out of the blue. He had worked farmhorses but never ridden, nor had his wife, Mavis, or their two older children, Jennifer and Ian. But when their younger daughter, Gillian, was a child, a friend called in and suggested they buy her a pony. 'I said "never" but the following week this so-called friend came into the yard with a 12.2 h.h. pony.'

Gill was eight and had never ridden before. At first she was bucked off, but she eventually managed the 'little villain'. One day she decided to hack over to a local show. Her father came home from the office, heard about the development and he and Gill's mother went to investigate. Their daughter stuck out like a sore thumb in scruffy jeans and top beside the jackets and jodhpurs of her rivals. However, she was just as keen as they were, so her parents bought her the proper gear. At the next show she looked the part, but the pony threw her. It was time to get her a better one.

She graduated to show ponies, where she met Clare Barr and they became firm friends. Both girls were winners in this field. Then Gill took a fancy to show jumping and her father bought a four-year-old called Prince's Pride, who initially looked very rough compared with the miniature Thoroughbred-types she had shown. The mare soon improved and was a winner both as a jumper and as a working hunter pony. Gill decided she preferred show jumping and, as she went round the shows, she and John became friends.

As Gill made the difficult transition from ponies to horses, she, John and Clare often met at shows and socially. After a few false starts, Gill gained a couple of good horses. When these reached Grade A, Rebound and Saint Mungo were bought as novices to school on in their wake. John went with Gill and her father to see both horses and advised them to buy.

Gill decided to retire from show jumping on a high note after reaching the 1982 Foxhunter Championship at Wembley with Rebound. She became credit controller for her father's company. Mr Brown could have sold the horses and backed out of show jumping, but by then both he and his wife were hooked. And because of the long-standing friendship with John, plus his prowess, he was the obvious candidate to take over the horses.

The Browns knew that John's approach to show jumping suited them. The horses were never ill-treated and the results were achieved naturally. After a round he was always happy to explain what had happened. Mrs Brown reckoned she did not know much about the sport, but John would make things clear without making her feel she knew nothing. His sincerity was also a bonus: whatever he said, he meant. The family relationship was cemented back in 1980 when Gill became godmother to John and Clare's daughter, Louise. When Gill married in 1984 Louise did her first bridesmaid's duty.

Although both Mr Barr and Mr Brown ran businesses which could have benefited from commercial plugs through John's show jumping success, both chose to keep the sport a purely private hobby. The horses were looked on as pets, not investments. Mr Barr once turned down an offer from a Dutchman of £80,000 for Ryan's Son. Mr Brown also refused huge offers for Saint Mungo, Rebound and even the pair. Other would-be buyers approached brandishing cheque books and saying, 'Name your price.' All three horses cost only the price of a good hunter; the profit resisted was several hundred per cent.

The private enthusiasts are in the sport for fun. In return for what they put in they gain immeasurable benefits to do with the joy of success and even the fascination of discussing misfortune. The personal interest brings stability to the owner-rider relationship and the possibility of long-term support. However, once a company parts with its money to a sportsman, it may want to justify its investment with hard figures about the favourable impact on sales, as it would do with other forms of advertising. For the show jumper the delivery of publicity as well as clear rounds and rosettes is an unaccustomed role. There is also the fear that the commercial link will force the rider to forfeit amateur status and with it an Olympic chance.

Amateur status is automatically lost if the company

wants its name incorporated in the horse's name for maximum publicity. This device can create cumbersome verbiage, or bring about a complete change in the horse's name, causing loss of identity and making the sport less romantic for the animal-loving British public. Commercial sponsorship may also be short term, allowing a stable to expand and then leaving it over-committed when the tap is turned off.

Next, the fast-growing fashion shop company, was not the first to offer sponsorship to John, but it was the first to come up with a deal which avoided most of the problems. The offer appealed because it was a nice idea to back both John and Michael, because the firm showed an understanding of the sport and because there was no threat to amateur status. The arrangement was for the brothers to lease their top horses to Next, initially for a total of £60,000 for the year leading up to the Los Angeles Olympics. This meant the horses, including Ryan's Son and Saint Mungo, would be referred to as belonging to Next – which did involve the actual owners putting up with a loss of prestige and some confusion.

For John, the main benefit of his £30,000 share was that it enabled some of the stable's expenses to be covered before the business of chasing prize money started. 'It relieved the pressure to win to pay for the horses' keep.' This meant the top performers could be paced over the season, bringing long-term benefits for the horses' health and attitude. While the established ones took it easy, younger horses could gain more county show experience, easing their introduction to Grade A classes. And when a lot of money was offered for one of the stable's rising stars it could be turned down without regret over the bills it might have paid.

The link between John and Michael Whitaker and Next was provided by British Equestrian Promotions, a London company with BBC commentator Raymond Brooks Ward as managing director. BEP deals mainly in finance for competitions, but it has also helped a few individual riders. In 1983 it handled about £1.5 million in sponsorship from more than forty firms.

BEP was already looking out for a sponsor for John and Michael when the inquiry came in from Next. A key factor in the ten weeks of negotiation was finding a formula which ensured the brothers stayed amateur, as the Olympics were only a year away. The arrangement worked out was that the £60,000 went into a trust fund administered by the British Equestrian Federation. It could only be paid out to John and Michael to cover expenses; there was to be no fee for their riding.

The brothers could not wish to have a more successful company behind them. Next was launched in February 1982, and by April 1985 had opened about 300 Next and Next For Men shops in Britain. Managing director George Davies said the firm's initial aim was to get involved in supporting Britain's Olympic effort for Los Angeles. Next plumped for show jumping because it was a favourite sport among women. 'We thought it would be of interest both to our customers and to the girls who work in the shops.' Providing an enjoyable association for staff and everyone else connected with Next was a major consideration.

At first Next thought of sponsoring a lady rider, but with the Olympics in mind John and Michael seemed the best prospects. Mr Davies, himself a TV fan of the sport, knew the brothers were household names and felt their 'nice guy' reputation would reflect well on the company. He felt the impact on sales would not be measurable and only a low-key commercial spin-off was expected. The emphasis was on intangible gains in terms of image and goodwill.

Next was clearly happy with the way the arrangement worked out, for in 1984, before the Olympics, the company agreed to extend the support for John and Michael. Each of the brothers was to receive £30,000 a year for the next two years, the same amount as they had received for 1983–4. Once again the owners of John and Michael's best horses agreed to lease them to Next, which meant that their names would be left out of show announcements.

However, one couple who had supported John since 1981, Charles and Betsy Newton, were not keen on giving up their rights. John had ridden Clonee Temple and Charlie's

Angel for them and in 1984 there were discussions over whether he would have the ride on Blue Moon, a nine-year-old Irish-bred grey gelding, who, ridden by Pauline Wakefield, had been well-placed in the Cock o' the North Championship and the Queen Elizabeth II Cup in 1983.

The Newtons had bought both Charlie's Angel and Blue Moon as grade As from Sir Hugh Fraser, whose daughter, Patricia, rode them in Scotland. Clonee Temple had been bought as a Grade B. Mr and Mrs Newton felt they had put a lot of money, time and effort into the sport, and were not keen to see a company waft in to take some of the credit and prestige. When their name flashed up on the TV screen they knew folks back in County Durham would sit up and take an interest and it was of benefit to Mr Newton's scrap processing business for the name to be publicized. They had to weigh up the disadvantages against the advantages of having their favourite rider on their horses. Above all they were keen to participate in the sport at the top level.

Mrs Newton had learned to ride after their marriage – not deterred by a fall from a racehorse or by the strange looks she got when she turned up for her first proper lesson in a sophisticated trouser suit and high heels. She soon got the hang of things and bought a hunter. It was when the groom took the hunter to a couple of local shows and came back with rosettes that Mr and Mrs Newton decided to go along to see what was happening. They enjoyed keeping their horses at home and producing them with the help of the rider. However, Clonee Temple and Charlie's Angel were kept at John's yard during their respective jumping seasons. The Newtons chose him because of his sympathetic riding and the way he avoided upsetting horses, which suited their affectionate view of their animals. It was a dilemma for the Newtons whether to plump for John with Next or find another rider. However, during 1984 they agreed that Clonee Temple should be part of the Next arrangement and it was also hoped that Blue Moon would join the stable.

The problem has long-term implications for the sport because both private enthusiasts and commercial sponsors are vital to keep the riders supplied with horses and help pay the bills. A formula is needed which gives credit to both types of supporter, but for riders who wish to remain amateur it has to avoid combining the firm's name with that of the horse.

A possible way of doing it would be to have the rider sponsored by the firm while the horse remained in the owner's name. On the TV screen it could look like this:

JOHN WHITAKER, sponsored by Next and Next® on
BLUE MOON, owned by Mrs E. B. Newton

Of course, it could not be guaranteed that writers and broadcasters would refer to both sponsor and owner in every story. But over the season each would receive plenty of mentions.

Just as important as those providing finance are the people who help with the work. The ever-growing demand for John's services as a rider enabled his string of horses to grow from half a dozen, when he and Clare moved into Heyside Farm in 1979, to fifteen by 1985. To help care for them all, they built up a team of four permanent staff – three grooms and one rider. Two of the girls, Angie Padfield and Karen Dyson, started work as school leavers in John's parents' yard. His father would put an advertisement in the local newspaper and take the first youngster who turned up. He did not expect them to know anything and they received no pay for the first few weeks while they were learning. If they stuck that baptism of fire, there was a good chance they would have the dedication required. Mandy Thomas had a couple of show jumping ponies whom she kept at the Whitakers' yard. When she left school she decided to make horses her career.

A groom's hours are long, the pay is modest and it is usually essential to live in. However, those who love horses and enjoy travelling the show circuit derive great satisfaction, especially when their charges win. They cover a wide variety of duties, from mucking out to riding, and they must be knowledgeable and conscientious enough to work with little supervision. John and Clare have to rely on them, particularly when they are away. If something is wrong with a horse, the groom must decide whether to act or bring in the boss. At home they look after four or five horses each and those are the ones with whom they form a special relationship.

Because of the skill, the vocational element and the variety, it compares well with other jobs open to unqualified girl school leavers. Their pay is all pocket money because their food and home are provided, making it an easy transition for a youngster leaving the family nest for the first time. John and Clare treat the grooms with respect and the relationship is friendly.

However, it is not surprising that the girls sometimes feel the grass must be greener elsewhere. When Mandy got the chance of a job as a shop assistant, late in 1983, when the morning frosts were beginning to bite at the snowline stables, she decided to try the apparently easier life. But within a few months she was back, having tried a couple of jobs and found them dull and less rewarding than working as a groom. She had missed the horses and John and Clare, for her work was bound to be far more valued in their small hard-working team than it was in unskilled 9 a.m. to 5 p.m. work that anyone could do.

Alan Fazakerley came to assist John in the winter of 1980–81. John had decided the previous summer, his first at Heyside Farm, that he needed a deputy. He was jumping a string of Grade As and the novices he had hoped to bring on were idling at home. He started looking for a likely youngster and his friend, Geoffrey Billington, introduced him to fellow Lancastrian Alan, then eighteen. He had worked at a show jumping yard since leaving school and was ready to move to a better place. Alan started off riding novices, but soon proved himself ready to take on Grade A and B horses. He regularly rode Hopscotch, Saint Mungo and Rebound during their rise through the grades.

8

On Course for the Games

Early in 1983 the British Show Jumping Association's team selectors called together a group of amateur riders to tell them informally that they were possibilities for the Olympics at Los Angeles. They would be watched through the coming season and the best would go on a short-list to be announced in the autumn. It also meant that if they were offered sponsorship, they should take care the arrangement left them amateurs. The meeting was of special relevance to John and Michael Whitaker, who were already key figures in the Olympic stakes, more than eighteen months before they actually jumped at Los Angeles.

John was then ranked third in the riders' league behind two professionals, Malcolm Pyrah and Nick Skelton. Ryan had won £35,000 the previous season, a total only bettered by Malcolm Pyrah's ride, Towerlands Anglezarke. Michael was ranked fifth, the second amateur, and his best horse in 1982, Disney Way, had totted up £19,970 combined national and international winnings – in the national league he was number one. The selectors' first task would be to pick out the most likely Olympic riders; the more thorny problem of what horses they rode at L.A. would have to be left until later. As with the other amateurs, there were many more question marks over John and Michael's prospective Olympic mounts than over their riding ability.

It was impossible then for John to say whether Ryan would remain at his peak until mid-1984, which would be his twelfth season of show jumping. By the end of 1982 Ryan had represented Britain more often than any other horse. To be considered for the Olympics eight years after he was first short-listed, and four years after he had competed at the Substitute Games, was a remarkable feat. Even if Ryan was still fit, John asked himself whether it would be fair to push him to new limits at the age of sixteen, and whether there was a risk that the Games would finish the horse's career abruptly and cruelly after such loyal service.

However, the Olympics were a long time ahead and John was in no doubt about his immediate goal: the 1983 European Championships at Ryan's favourite ground, Hickstead. With this in mind he worked out a programme so that the veteran campaigner would peak for that event, from 27 to 31 July.

His plan was to jump him at Easter in the British World Cup qualifier at Birmingham, go on to the last European qualifier in Sweden and then the final itself in Vienna. Ryan would then take May and June easy before his big build-up started at the Royal Show, Warwickshire, in the first week of July. In the early summer John would concentrate on British shows with his other grade A horses.

It all made absolute sense to John and the programme appeared to go like clockwork. At his first major outing at Birmingham, in the World Cup qualifier, Ryan was so exuberant at returning to the spotlight that he threw an enormous buck on the approach to a double of uprights, each more than 5 feet high. As John tried to control him, he broke down to a trot but still popped cleanly over both parts. He went on to win the competition with the only three clear rounds, beating the best European competition. Ryan was fourth in the Gothenburg qualifier which, added to the points gained earlier in the indoor season by Clonee Temple, put John top of the European League. In the American-dominated final, only a couple of unlucky 4-fault rounds prevented John coming higher than tenth. But the main thing was that Ryan had come back from his winter rest as brilliant as ever. With that established, John felt his horse had nothing more to prove to the selectors, and he went ahead with his plan to slacken him off until July.

83

And he stuck to this regime despite pressure to take Ryan to Aachen, West Germany, at the end of June. The dilemma was whether to chase the prestigious shows to impress the selectors, but risk a stale horse, or to keep religiously to what he knew was best for Ryan and ask the powers to trust him. He kept telling them Ryan would be at his peak for the Championships.

For the selectors the problem was that Ryan's summer campaign did not start until the Royal Show, less than forty-eight hours before they had to name the European Championship team. What John did not know was that one or two key people had formed the opinion, at the World Championships at Dublin the previous year, that Ryan was past his best. After all, it was normal for a horse to decline in his teens. Of course, Ryan was not normal, but the selectors were not prepared to believe that, without inspecting his performance at international shows in 1983. Memories of his win at Birmingham faded fast – the selectors were anyway inclined to put much less weight on wins indoors.

The other factor was that John's rivals, the professionals David Broome, Malcolm Pyrah, Harvey Smith and Nick Skelton, had won the Paris Nations Cup in mid-June. The importance of this victory was amplified because it wreaked vengeance on the French for the sound beating they had given the British team at Hickstead in May. In the process, David Broome and Harvey Smith had shown that their international experience could make up for the inexperience of their mounts.

The selection committee comprised four riders, David Broome, Malcolm Pyrah, Graham Fletcher and Peter Robeson, team manager Ronnie Massarella, and four of the sport's long-standing amateur officials. The chairman was ex-international show jumper General Sir Cecil Blacker.

When the decision day came during the Royal Show, where John and Ryan's Son had already achieved a second placing, they went for the conservative option of sticking with the winning team from Paris. The chosen ones were the two top horse-and-rider combinations, Malcolm Pyrah on Towerlands Anglezarke and Nick Skelton on St James.

84

plus former World Champion David Broome on his up-and-coming horse, Last Resort and Harvey Smith on either his Paris mount, Sanyo Technology, or another improving horse, Sanyo Olympic Video. John was described as missing selection 'by a whisker'.

John was not surprised, but he was angry. He had had a feeling he would be left out because he had disobeyed the selectors' wishes in shunning the chance to go to Aachen. He was told that Ryan had not shown top-class form before the selection date. He replied that Ryan had not jumped anywhere to do that and that the horse did not need to prove himself yet again. He had stuck to his guns so that the horse would be right for the Championships. He had never been so sure that Ryan was coming to his peak at just the right time. He had told the selectors that. 'But they must have thought I was a dumbo because they did not listen.'

His disappointment was exacerbated because Ryan had limited time left at the top and John wanted him to have another chance at something big. He also wondered whether he would ever have another horse as good to give him such high hopes of Championship medals. 'I was much more mad about being left out of that team than I was over missing the Olympics in 1976, when I had known in the back of my mind that Ryan was not yet ready.' Not that John attacked the selectors. He realized they had a difficult job and credited them with picking the team they thought had the best chance of winning. In 1984, when John was a certainty for the Olympics, the selectors told him to prepare Ryan just as he wanted. John took this as recognition that he had been right the previous year.

Ryan's light introduction to the 1983 season, which had spared him a period of jumping on very hard ground, stood him in good stead for July's major shows and he strung together an impressive set of results. He got into the jump-off nearly every time out, but then if he went clear again others would go faster; if he had a fast 4 faults, someone would beat him with a slow clear. On the last day of the Royal, he was runner-up to Jeff McVean in the National

Championship (although Jeff was Australian, he still took the title because he was based in Britain). At the Great Yorkshire John was second to Malcolm Pyrah in the Cock o' the North Championship and Malcolm pipped him again on the first night of the Royal International Horse Show.

However, it was on the hallowed ground of the White City, where the Royal International returned in 1983 after fifteen years at Wembley, that John's luck changed. Nostalgia surrounded the move. The stadium had been the Royal International's home for more than twenty years. David Broome and Harvey Smith had jumped into the limelight there, challenging the previous generation – Harry Llewellyn, Pat Smythe and Wilf White – who were then at the zenith of their powers.

At the age of twenty-seven, making his first appearance at the White City, John had some important points to prove with Ryan's Son. After two weeks of performances as good as any other British rider, he needed to show that he could also beat the best in Europe. He wanted to squash any doubts about Ryan's continuing ability and he was anxious to end his run of second places with a resounding victory. If he could achieve all this, he would have shown the selectors exactly what they had missed. An added factor was that he would like to add his name to the historic roll of White City winners. As it was, history was to take a dramatic turn which would give him his chance at the European Championships.

The show's blue riband event was the King George V Gold Cup, one of the most coveted prizes in show jumping. Neither John nor his friend, Nick Skelton – bound for the Championships the following week – had won it. Disaster struck Nick early in the course; he was approaching a high upright which, under the floodlights, cast an ominous shadow. He felt St James look at a nearby camera. The horse never took off properly, knelt on the fence and then nose-dived. His forelegs failed to stretch out for landing and he crumpled and rolled.

When St James rose, Nick saw a sickening gash on the outside of the horse's knee. He galloped away, not obviously lame, but it was inevitable that pain and stiffness would set in. Nick's mentor, Ted Edgar, rushed the horse home to Warwickshire that night and some thirty stitches were put in the wound. The other part of the prescription was complete rest. John was not immediately aware that Nick's fall had catapulted him into the European Championships. He was concerned for his friend, who was unhurt, but his first task was the King's Cup.

Ryan sensed the big occasion and as John walked up to him prior to the competition he started dancing about and delivered a few of his notorious headbutts. He was in fine form and made light of the uneven going, which a faulty watering system had made partly boggy, partly hard. Ryan was one of five British clears. The only foreign combination in the jump-off was reigning European Champion Paul Schockemöhle, from West Germany, with Deister. Schockemöhle was the first to go in the first jump-off, which was not against the clock. He was clear again and remained the only one with a clean sheet. John just had the last fence down for equal second place with Malcolm Pyrah.

After the competition John had time to turn over the idea that he might be going to the European Championships after all. Apart from St James's accident, he also knew that David Broome's horse, Last Resort, had been pulled out of the Royal International with a sore foot. With two horses doubtful, he knew his chance was rekindled.

St James's withdrawal from the Championships was confirmed the day after the King's Cup. A selection meeting, arranged months before the upset, suddenly had an extra item on the agenda. The proceedings, which were in private, dragged on. However, the decision to include John and Ryan in the team, as a replacement for Nick Skelton and St James, did not take long. The only other rider in contention was Liz Edgar, but Everest Forever had not been on his best form and John was chosen unopposed.

Despite his dreadful luck at missing the Championships, Nick did not begrudge John his chance. He thought it unfair that John had been left out originally, when he had a horse which had never let a team down. He wished John luck and

87

said he could think of no better person to take his place. He still had a slim chance of being selected on Maybe, as a replacement for Last Resort, who did not recover in time from his lameness. However, the selectors preferred to keep David Broome in on his second string, Mr Ross.

After all this political turmoil, what John really needed was a win to set the seal on his Championship build-up. Ryan obliged in the richest competition of the week at the White City, taking the John Player Grand Prix, worth £3,550 to the winner. The competition had looked as though it would develop into a steeplechase after the first round, when fifteen were clear. But the first jump-off over a few massive fences, not against the clock, really sorted them out. Among the failures – showing that horses are never machines – were Towerlands Anglezarke and Deister. Five went through to the timed jump-off, including Nick on Maybe, who was first to go. He had 4 faults in a fast time and the next to go, World Champion Norbert Koof, on Fire went slower but still had one down.

John knew a neat clear would put pressure on the remaining two and he struck a perfect balance between taking no foolhardy risks and wasting no time. Trying to beat his target, both David Bowen, the eventual runner up, and Lesley McNaught made mistakes. John was the outright winner, the only one to jump three clear rounds.

Although it had taken a twist of fate to let John into the European Championships, his plan to bring Ryan to a peak for that event had worked perfectly. The stiff courses and hotly contested jumps-off, in which he had been for the past three weeks, had made him super fit and prepared for any type of obstacle. Mentally Ryan was more settled than at the earlier shows, where his exuberance had created unwanted problems for John. However, most importantly he was still fresh, enjoying his jumping and willing to make the extra effort to clear the big fences.

As far as John was concerned, his mental preparation would have been 100 per cent had he been picked for the team the first time round. But the goad of having to prove his point to the selectors – who had picked him as second best – sent his motivation into overdrive.

* * * *

The European Championships were the showpiece of the 1983 season. Silk Cut sponsored the Championship classes to the tune of £35,000, but this time it was the quest for gold, silver and bronze medals which drew the cream of Europe's show jumpers. Thirteen countries sent teams of four riders, including the reigning European Champions, West Germany, and the reigning World Champions, France. The individual European and World Champions, Paul Schockemöhle and Norbert Koof, were both in the West German squad. But the team on top form was Switzerland, who had won the Aachen Nations Cup.

Hickstead, in Sussex, is Britain's only permanent outdoor show jumping arena with the wealth of materials and space needed to mount world-class events. The man behind it is Douglas Bunn, a former international rider, who decided in the late 1950s that British riders needed practice over the more imposing type of course they would have to negotiate on the continent. The distinguishing features include natural obstacles, which are more like the ones a horse would meet across country than in a conventional British show ring. Also the spreads are wider and there is more filling between the poles and the ground. These unaccustomed features can make even the boldest horse back off at his first encounter.

Mr Bunn masterminded the building of the showground on land at his home, just off the A23 London to Brighton Road. The international arena measures 180 yards by 140 yards and is famed for the quality of its turf and shrubs and for its ornamental lake, as well as for the high standard of competition. It attracts up to 30,000 people to the biggest events and a few million more enjoy the contests on television. And they were in for a treat at the end of July 1983 as the European Championship contenders took to the International Arena.

The race for both team and individual titles started with

a speed class, which is not Ryan's favourite type of competition. Most of the fences were a shade under 5 feet and each one knocked down added 7 seconds to the competitor's total time. The course was not difficult and the riders had to take time-saving risks to reach the top ten individual placings and boost their team's chances. The Swiss riders, Walter Gabathuler and Willi Melliger, gave scorching displays of speed and accuracy to take first and second places. Their team mate, Thomas Fuchs, was also clear for sixth place, which gave the Swiss team a two-fence lead.

David Broome, three times winner of the European title, was the only member of the home team to jump clear, and he finished in seventh place. John knew he had to cut corners to clock a fast time on Ryan, who is not built for speed. But at one fence, a wide triple bar, Ryan anticipated the turn and John had to make the best of a very short run. Ryan took off a bit far from the fence and dropped a hindleg on the middle pole. It was a risk that could have come off, but it left John in thirteenth place. Malcolm Pyrah had a fast time, despite one down, on Towerlands Anglezarke, and the British team was in the silver medal position after the first competition.

For the climax of the Team Championship the next day, the fences were raised to about 5 feet 3 inches for a gruelling two-round, Nations Cup-style competition. The best three scores from the four team members would count in each round and be added to the running totals from the previous day's speed class. John was first to go for the British team and had 4 faults at a comparatively easy parallel. He was annoyed with himself for letting Ryan lose his rhythm round the preceding corner and for finding him a long flat stride into the fence.

Things did not look good for the British team when Harvey Smith had 20 faults on the inexperienced Sanyo Olympic Video; the West Germans were on their tail and the Swiss were still on song for gold. Fortunately, Malcolm Pyrah and David Broome revived our hopes with clears and David Broome temporarily moved into the individual bronze medal position. Gabathuler was still in the lead, with Schockemöhle breathing down his neck.

In the second round John gave the team just the start it needed with a clear. Then Harvey Smith conjured a fault-less round out of Olympic Video with inch-perfect judge-ment at every fence. Malcolm Pyrah's 4 faults clinched the silver for Britain, the Swiss stayed two fences ahead to take gold and West Germany won the bronze. Ironically, the speed class proved the deciding factor. Each of the top three had a total of 8 faults after the two-round competition, and in a Nations Cup they would have jumped off against the clock. This time the first day scores, over a lower course, made the difference.

In the Individual Championship, David Broome dropped down the order following an 8 fault round at the end of the Team Championship. John and Malcolm Pyrah moved up to ninth and seventh places, respectively. However, less than one fence separated John from five of the riders lying ahead of him.

The final part of the individual competition was a two-round contest over the biggest courses of the week. The fences were well over 5 feet high and up to 6 feet 7 inches wide. In the lead was the reigning champion, Schock-emöhle, on Deister, the only one in the competition yet to have a fence down. Within striking distance of him was Walter Gabathuler, but Schockemöhle had a fence in hand over Willi Melliger in third place. The thirty riders jumped in reverse order of their placings.

When John came into the arena there were no clears, but he knew the best horses were still to come. He jumped the first clear round, putting pressure on those above him. The next three, Frédéric Cottier, from France, Malcolm Pyrah and the Austrian, Hugo Simon, kept their cool and also returned clear rounds. But the leading group crumbled, the three Swiss riders each having three fences down and a West German hitting four. John moved up to fifth place and Malcolm Pyrah was in the bronze medal position. Schockemöhle went clear again, giving him two fences in hand over Simon, his nearest rival, but less than one fence separated John from the little Austrian on Gladstone.

The second round was over a shorter course of even bigger obstacles and included a double of lightweight white rails, designed to catch out the horses flagging after three days of strenuous competition. This time a few had jumped clear by the time it was John's turn. He could have lost hope of a medal at that stage, believing that the world-class horses in front of him just would not make mistakes. But he knew the fickleness of show jumping fortunes better than that and was determined to capitalize on it. Only two competitors lay between him and a medal.

He jumped a second clear, which took him into the lead. Then he had to watch in suspense while the next four rounds decided the outcome. It was hard work waiting, but there was nothing more he could do.

First to crack was Frédéric Cottier on Flambeau C, who was only 5/100 of a point ahead of John. He made one mistake, at a big spread fence. Malcolm Pyrah and Hugo Simon knocked down both parts of the double of white rails, losing their medal positions and putting John in line for the silver. The impeccable Deister kept his clean sheet in his fifth round of jumping to give Paul Schockemöhle the individual title, although he did have a time fault. John was the only competitor in the last contest with a double clear.

In the midst of his pride at winning the silver medal, John also retained an objective, almost modest, view of the achievement. He said he had had nothing to lose and everything to gain on the last day of the Championships. He had already acquitted himself well in the team event and, coming from ninth place for the individual, he was in no danger of throwing away a medal chance. 'It was the leaders who had a lot to lose that day and there was more pressure on them than me. I would like to say that I could have stayed as cool if I had been in front rather than coming from behind. I don't know, it was easier for me.'

Among onlookers the talk was suddenly of John and Ryan

as the anchor combination in the British team for the Los Angeles Olympics the following year.

* * * *

At the end of August John turned his mind to the class which meant nearly as much to him as winning an Olympic gold medal, the Jumping Derby at Hickstead. It was being held on the Sunday of the Bank Holiday meeting, and was sponsored by Hambro Life Assurance. The first prize was the richest in Europe, £14,000, but the money was less significant than the prestige attached to jumping a clear round. In the previous twenty-two Derbys only sixteen horses had managed clears, among them some of the best show jumpers of all time: Goodbye (Seamus Hayes), Flanagan (Pat Smythe), Stroller (Marion Mould), The Maverick (Alison Dawes), Mister Softee (David Broome) and Boomerang (Eddie Macken).

John had had 4 faults on Ryan's Son in each of the previous three Derbys, gaining two equal seconds and a fourth. His nearest miss had come in 1980 when his brother, Michael, then only twenty, had jumped clear on Owen Gregory. Ryan had just clipped the last of the sixteen fences on the ¾ mile course. In 1982 he was one of eight horses with 4 faults involved in a jump-off against the clock. On that occasion the class was won by Paul Schockemöhle on Deister.

The Derby course is the same every year, which enhances its epic quality. Several of the fences are 5 feet 3 inches high and the spreads are up to 6 feet 7 inches. Sixteen fences in a course is forty per cent more than the average competition; the fact that five of the fences are combinations means that the horse has to make a total of twenty-three efforts. The actual ground covered is about twice as far as usual and the horse has to keep up a steady 15 m.p.h. to keep within the 3-minute time allowed. Most arenas have a water jump, but outside Hickstead horses very rarely see ditches, banks or drops. On the Derby course thirteen obstacles incorporate one of these 'natural' features.

Before the 1983 meeting Ryan had had a three-week rest

from jumping following his silver successes at the European Championships – and the anticlimax of an unnecessary trip to Dublin. Meanwhile, John had competed at Rotterdam, gaining some good placings on Mr and Mrs Newton's promising grey gelding, Blue Moon. John had also taken Saint Mungo for some much-needed international experience, but instead the horse ended up the victim of a mysterious accident. He was discovered one morning with blood all round his stable. The source was a 5 inch long cut in his mouth, which was still bleeding profusely. No one knew how it had happened. The vet stemmed the flow and the injury turned out to be less serious than at first feared. Back at home the wound healed quickly and Mungo was fit enough to join Ryan, Charlie's Angel and San Salvador for the trip to Hickstead.

Because Ryan was short of work John took him in two classes before Derby day for a school. The old horse was rather headstrong and had a fence down in the Derby Trial and hit two on the eve of the big event. However, his stable mates excelled themselves. Charlie's Angel was runner up in the Derby Trial to Disney Way, ridden by Michael Whitaker. And the following day Mungo won his first big class in the international arena. On Salvador John made an embarrassing start, getting eliminated for missing out a fence. He redeemed himself later in the meeting by notching up two seconds on the smart little chestnut.

Ryan's performances had been mediocre, but John was not worried. His sights were set on the Derby and he had put no pressure on Ryan in the previous competitions. 'He will be right tomorrow,' he said.

John retains as much respect now for the track as at his first attempt in 1977. He always walks it twice, planning his approach to each obstacle so that his horse will have the best chance of going clear. Number one, a solid wall called 'the Cornishman', is the only fence John describes as 'nice'. The second is a parellel of white poles over spruce, too wide to be taken casually. Next comes the first really difficult test, the double of water ditches. Each part consists of high upright poles standing behind about 5 feet of water.

94

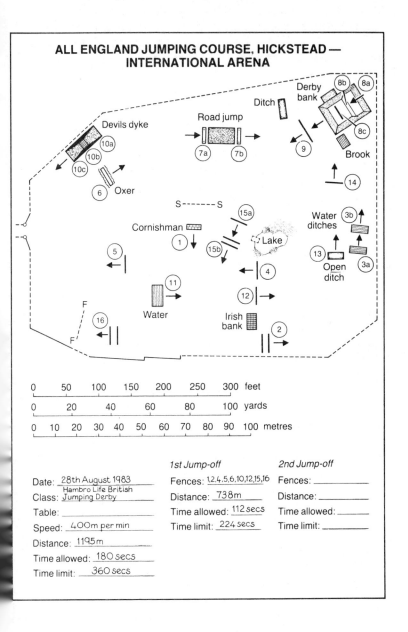

**ALL ENGLAND JUMPING COURSE, HICKSTEAD —
INTERNATIONAL ARENA**

Date: 28th August 1983
Class: Hambro Life British Jumping Derby
Table: _____
Speed: 400m per min
Distance: 1195m
Time allowed: 180 secs
Time limit: 360 secs

1st Jump-off
Fences: 1,2,4,5,6,10,12,15,16
Distance: 738m
Time allowed: 112 secs
Time limit: 224 secs

2nd Jump-off
Fences: _____
Distance: _____
Time allowed: _____
Time limit: _____

95

at which the horses tend to spook, and there is a long stride between the fences so that the horses have to take off further away than usual. After that the next two, a gate and a wall, are 'normal', despite their height of 5 feet 3 inches.

Before the next obstacle, a 6 feet 6 inches wide spread over a privet hedge, the horses have to turn away from the collecting ring and some lose their rhythm. The parallel is imposing and a few horses, mistaking the hedge for a bank, dangerously drop their legs in the middle. At fence seven, the 'table', there is a ditch behind the first part and another in front of the second, which also has a drop on landing. John prefers to push on for three strides over the raised ground in between. 'If you fiddle for four, you may end up in the hole.'

Next is the infamous Derby Bank, approached from the far corner of the ring. The horse climbs up a terraced slope and quickly meets a small upright on top, over which it has to trot. 'If you go too fast, you must start flapping your arms,' says John, standing on the edge of the precipice. The 10 feet descent of the bank is nearly vertical. The horse should jump off it about 3 feet from the bottom, ready for an upright only 11 yards away; there is only room for two strides.

The three-part Devil's Dyke, which follows, involves a drop on the way in, a water ditch in the sunken middle and an uphill effort to jump out. There is just one stride between each fence. As the horse approaches he can see the water glinting below between the sparse rustic poles. This obstacle usually catches out most of the field. John says a bold jump in is necessary, but the risk is that the horse will not get high enough at the first part.

The water jump follows, with only a white bar in front instead of the usual brush, making it more difficult to judge. Then the rider has to steady the pace for high rustic planks, which are all too easy to dislodge. If the horse has got this far, the next dry ditch should raise few problems, despite its grave-like appearance.

Now the horses start to tire and for some the next 5 feet

3 inches upright is too much. Then comes the turn for home and a gruelling uphill run to a double of gates. The second one has a 5 feet 6 inch spread and tired horses, or ones jumping in too slowly, tend to hit the back bar. The last spread fence caught John out in 1980, when he was equal second behind his brother Michael; he now makes sure the horse is paying full attention as he turns towards it.

Throughout the three-minute test the rider must concentrate totally and sustain the horse's rhythm. The obstacles must be attacked and there is no room for a lack of determination.

As he walked from the ring on 28 August 1983, John started to muster all his resources. If he could go clear, he would be only the fifteenth rider to do so. Only twenty-one clear rounds had been jumped in twenty-two years. Seamus Hayes, Marion Mould, Alison Dawes, Harvey Smith and Eddie Macken were the only ones to have done it more than once.

A crowd of more than 20,000 flocked to the international arena, eagerly awaiting the afternoon spectacle. Several scores of them, clutching autograph books, milled around below the building where the riders go to watch the competitions. They stood three or four deep across the entrance to the practice area, admiring the horses gathering under the trees and trying to tell which rider was which. They were treated to an informal jumping demonstration as competitors early in the order started to warm up.

The pre-contest pomp and ceremony primed the emotions of every onlooker as the grand parade of riders circled the arena, their hats off in salute as the Welsh Guards played the national anthem of each competing nation: Austria, Ireland, West Germany and Britain. The twenty home riders, in ranks of four, got a tremendous patriotic cheer.

The suspense was thoroughly wound up by the time the first to jump, James Kernan, from Ireland, entered the arena. He had 11 faults at two of the bogey fences, the bank and the Devil's Dyke. There followed two disastrous rounds before one of the oldest horses in the competition, seven-

97

teen-year-old Hydrophane Coldstream, ridden by Derek Ricketts, showed the way with just 4 faults.

John's first attempt was on Charlie's Angel, eighteenth to go. He had watched the first ten rounds, which included two eliminations, three cricket scores and one fall. A few nerves fluttered, but he knew that would help by increasing his adrenalin and determination. As he worked in the grey mare, who had been placed the previous year with an 8 fault round, Harvey Smith joined Derek Ricketts in the lead. Harvey, who had won the class four times, must have been kicking himself for hitting the second fence, one of the lowest on the course.

Charlie jumped the first five fences well, but was momentarily disunited on the turn towards the privet oxer, losing vital rhythm. She hit the front pole. On the Derby bank she slipped right to the bottom and could not recover in time to jump the following fence, which she refused and then cleared. Two parts of the Devil's Dyke also fell, making a total of 15 faults.

There were ten more to go before John and Ryan, including two former winners, Michael Whitaker on Owen Gregory, and Paul Schockemöhle on Deister. Michael's first ride, Disney Way, hit the oxer and one part of the Devil's Dyke, becoming the fourth horse to finish on 8 faults. Then a young rider on a veteran horse, Chris Parker and Rossmore, joined the other two 4-faulters. Already there was talk of a jump-off between those with just one mistake. This intensified as Deister lowered the first part of the Devil's Dyke and Owen Gregory had 8 faults. However, it gave Ryan the chance to win the competition outright.

Ryan entered the ring as fresh as a daisy and jumped the first two fences for fun. At the first bogey fence, the double of water ditches, he touched a pole. John had an anxious moment as he heard the knock, but nothing fell. After that Ryan jumped cleanly and the round followed John's model to the letter. The crowd held its breath as he popped off the bank, took two strides and took off at the perfect spot for the upright. At the Devil's Dyke Ryan just skimmed a pole on the way in, but was never in danger of dislodging it. He was the first to be clear so far round the course and the spectators burst into applause; Ryan responded with a buck. The worst was over. Water had never been a problem for Ryan and he made light of the exhausting final phase. He was clapped after every fence. Coming to the last, the memory of 1980, when that parallel had foiled his bid, flashed across John's mind. He collected Ryan and then sent him forward on a perfect stride.

As Ryan landed John's face broke into a great beam of delight. He swept off his hat and waved it in triumph at the crowd, who were on their feet cheering. Ryan joined in the ecstasy with a string of bucks.

It was the competition that John had always wanted to win. He was even more proud to don the blue sash of honour for the victory parade than he had been to bend his head for silver medals at the Substitute Olympics and the European Championships. Jumping a clear round over the classic course was just as important to him as the first prize.

The £14,000 prize money sent John to the top of the riders' league for the first time since the publication of the monthly computer list, which had started in spring 1982. Sixty British riders are listed and their scores are worked out by awarding one point for every £50 won on Grade A horses over the previous twelve months. For the year ending 31 August 1983, John's total was 1,809.94 points, the equivalent of £90,497, taking him past the long-time leader Malcolm Pyrah.

END OF TERM

The selectors were quick to reward John's form with Ryan's Son, and to put him on course for the Olympic Games, by sending him to the Calgary international show in Canada. His brother, Michael, was also chosen to represent Britain at this prestigious event, which boasted the world's richest show jumping prize – 35,000 Canadian dollars (about £20,000) to the winner of the du Maurier International. However, it was also a major test of the team, because among the countries contesting the Nations Cup would be the United States, already favourites to win the Olympic Gold medal on their home ground at Los Angeles. With John and Michael in the team were professionals Harvey Smith and Malcolm Pyrah.

John and Michael excelled themselves, Ryan jumping a double clear and Overton Amanda – in her first international season – having a clear and 4 faults. This helped the team to gain equal second place, with West Germany, behind the United States. It was these three teams which nearly a year later would share out the team show jumping medals at the Olympics. That performance in Calgary helped Britain to its tenth President's Cup win since 1965 – this is a trophy awarded annually to the country gaining the most points in six Nations Cups.

In the du Maurier International the following day a 'silly' fence in the second round cost John the £20,000 first prize. He was one of only five clears in the first round and a repetition would have won the class outright because the eventual winner, Norman Dello Joio, from the United States, finished with ½ time fault. John cleared the bogey fence, a treble, but he had already hit a comparatively small gate at number three. He ended up with the ninth prize of 2,000 dollars.

After the trip to Canada Ryan had a relaxing time before an event which everyone still regards as an end-of-term celebration, the Horse of the Year Show. It brings together the pick of British riders, from the senior internationals to the pony-riding teenagers. Each grade of horse has an end-of-season championship at Wembley and most of them come through two qualifying rounds to get there. About 130 riders qualify altogether, just one in 114 of the BSJA's 15,000 members. The international classes, with their generous prize money, also draw a foreign contingent to add spice to the already intense competition.

It was a milestone in John's career when, in 1971, he first qualified for Wembley for the Leading Junior Show Jumper of the Year final. The following two years he again qualified just one horse, Singing Wind, for one class – first the Foxhunter Championship for novice horses and then the Whitbread Young Riders final for riders aged eighteen and under. With Ryan's Son in 1974 he won enough money to qualify for all the major competitions and since then the number of horses qualifying each year from his stable has risen to six. Alan Fazakerley, who helped the horses clock up the required level of prize money, shared the rides with John.

Although most of the competitions leading up to Wembley were held out of doors on grassy showgrounds, the Horse of the Year Show has always been indoors. It marks both the end of the summer season and the beginning of the winter indoor circuit. A wooden floor is laid over the swimming lanes at the Empire Pool and a mixture of soil, peat and shavings provides the going. The arena measures 210 feet by 85 feet and would fit more than twelve times into the international ring at Hickstead.

Jumping indoors presents horse and rider with a few extra problems. Having fences close together – with related distances – and near to corners means the horse must be balanced on turns and maintain his impulsion no matter how tight the manoeuvre. The horse's schooling and obedience is severely tested; a moment's reluctance or a headstrong surge of speed will cause all sorts of problems on the short approach to the next fence. Because the jumps come up suddenly both rider and horse must think more quickly than when jumping outside, where there is more room to get organized. Strong horses, like Charlie's Angel, and long-striding ones, like Saint Mungo, are more difficult to ride in the confined space.

Another problem is that the horse can often tell which way he must turn on landing from a fence at the end of the arena. Over the years Ryan has learned the trick of anticipating turns and John always has to be ready to stop him cutting the corners because indoors this leaves an alarmingly short run to the next fence. The horses also have to become accustomed to floodlights and the serried tiers of spectators breathing over the edge of the arena, with about 60,000 people attending during the week. All these features add to the excitement and the only thing the riders do not like about the Horse of the Year Show is the cost of entering. In 1984 it cost the Whitaker stable about £500 for entries and stabling.

The Wembley arena is busy from dawn until midnight. As well as show jumping there are national finals for the best horses in every field of equestrian sport. The showing championships cater for ponies, hunters, hacks and cobs, the top six Pony Club mounted games teams fight out the Prince Philip Cup, police horses, dressage riders and the horse drivers all have plum titles to go for. There are traditional displays like the musical drive of the heavy horses and touches of sentiment. In 1983 a bravery award was presented to Sefton, the Household Cavalry horse who survived appalling injuries in the Hyde Park bombing the previous year.

The show jumpers join in the ceremony and the fun, as well as getting down to the serious business of competing. John can find himself taking part in a parade of medal winners one night and captaining a mock Pony Club team in gymkhana events the next. In the competitions Ryan has a tremendously consistent record, getting into most of the jump-offs, while John's back-up horses have brought him prizes in both puissance and speed classes.

John also enjoys the successes of his friends and family. In particular in 1983 his brother Steven, then aged twenty-six, jumped Take Your Pick in the Godfrey Davis Grade C Championship. Discussing his tactics with John, Steven's original plan for the jump-off was to do a steady clear but, after seeing his speedy rivals, that decision was revised to 'going like hell'. It came off, and Steven had the delight of doing his first victory lap under the famous Wembley spotlight. John's deputy rider, Alan Fazakerley, also made a bit of personal history at the 1983 show. It was the first time he had jumped for the full week at Wembley and his best result was a second on Saint Mungo in the Next Fashion Stakes, backed by John and Michael's sponsors. John won one class and was placed in several others, landing about £5,000 prize money.

102

A few years ago this would have been the end of the season, and the Grade As would have been roughed off until the end of the winter. They would have spent the days grazing, just coming in at night for protection from the worst of the weather, until the cycle restarted early the next year with gentle roadwork. Now there is the Christmas Show at Olympia to look forward to, continental qualifiers for the World Cup and a few prestigious winter shows in this country. This means that John has to stagger the programmes of his Grade A horses, so while some rest others are fully fit and fresh for competition.

The winter is also an important time at home for bringing on young horses. In between the international shows John goes to shows near home with plenty of novice classes, such as Rufforth Park, near Wetherby. The four-year-olds make their debuts in the ring over fences about 2 feet 6 inches high, in classes without a jump-off, where every clear round gets a rosette. As their confidence grows they start in Newcomers and Foxhunter competitions, where the fences are between 3 feet and 4 feet high.

The daily programme for these youngsters alternates schooling, practice jumping and roadwork. Since the winter of 1984–5 John has had a barn-cum-indoor school to use for training. One of his principles is to ensure young horses have plenty of variety to keep them interested in their lessons. When teaching them to jump, John makes plenty of use of trotting and take-off poles to regulate the novice's approach to the nursery fences. If he is trying it over a new obstacle, he often puts poles at the sides of the jump to discourage running out. 'I believe in prevention. It's better never to let them learn the wrong way,' he says. He does not mind if the horse makes mistakes, so long as there is improvement. It may hit a strange fence once with its fore-legs and once behind before clearing it. That's OK: 'He can only cope with one thing at a time, but with each jump he learns.' And this patient approach to each training session will have to be telescoped over three or four years before John will know whether a youngster has any prospect of emulating Ryan.

103

9

Olympic Build-Up

The Horse of the Year Show in 1983 marked the close of the last full season before the Los Angeles Olympics and, little more than a week after the final curtain at Wembley, the selectors were due to name the first short-list. This would leave them nine months to sort out five riders and up to eight horses for the trans-Atlantic trip. They were looking for riders capable of jumping the biggest courses the sport will allow, taking on the best competition in the world and shouldering the additional pressure of the Olympic phenomenon, especially in the team event.

On paper the dimensions of Olympic fences are the same as those in European or World Championships. For the team event and the first round of the individual contest, the rules say the height of the fences should be between 1.4 metres (4 feet 7 inches) and 1.6 metres (5 feet 3 inches), and the spreads should vary from 1.5 metres (4 feet 11 inches) to 2 metres (6 feet 7 inches), with an extra 20 centimetres width allowed for a sloping triple bar. The course should have between twelve and fifteen obstacles, including two or three combinations, and a water jump up to 4.75 metres (15 feet 7 inches) wide. The dimensions are even bigger for the second round of the individual championship. One upright and one spread must be 1.7 metres high (5 feet 7 inches) and the width of the spread can be 2 metres (6 feet 7 inches). The course can be raised again for a jump-off.

John had often jumped fences at 5 feet 3 inches, and occasionally one or two higher during a championship jump-off or a puissance. However, he knew there were ways

John *(left)* and Nick Skelton being brought down to size at Olympia, 1984

Memories of gymkhana days came flooding back to John as he led this Pony Club team
victory in a 'friendly' competition at the Horse of the Year Show, 1983

On the way to victory in the 1983 Hambro
Life Jumping Derby at Hickstead, John
and Ryan take the infamous Derby Bank
in their stride

Below left: Pause for thought during the
World Championships at Dublin in 1982

Below right: Ryan puts in one of his
devilish bucks during a schooling session
at John's farm

Right: John, Ryan and the horsebox
which publicizes the sponsoring compan
Next. The numbers on Ryan's back are a
freeze brand to guard against theft

One of John's team-mates at the 1984 Olympics in Los Angeles – Steven Smith on the Team Sanyo's Shining Example

They have every reason to be happy. The 1984 Olympic silver-medal winning squad (from the left): Steven Smith, team manager Ronnie Massarella, coach Peter Robeson, Tim Grubb, John Whitaker, David Bowen and Michael Whitaker

in which these dimensions could be used to make fences which were 'killers'. Not that the horse would die trying to clear them, but it might fall, refuse or be so frightened that its attitude to jumping would never be the same again. John could think of several good horses which had never regained their best form after the Olympics and he was wary of making a similar sacrifice of Ryan.

One way of increasing the difficulty would be to combine the maximum height and the maximum width in a true parallel. For a horse to clear two parallel poles at 5 feet 7 inches the peak of the bascule had to be several inches higher, and because 6 feet 7 inches was wider than British horses were used to, there was a risk of landing on the back bar. It would also be a formidable novelty to have most of the fences at 5 feet 3 inches, rather than just the occasional upright or staggered spread. Finally, the course builder could make the approach to these huge fences difficult by using trick distances. John ran the possibilities through his mind and conjured up a picture of a double of parallels, both of maximum size, with a long stride between them and a bad set of strides leading up to them!

Clearly riders with plenty of guts and experience would be needed and the best guide to that should have been the similarly gruelling courses at the most recent World and European Championships. But in Britain, when it came to the Olympics there was an extra constraint on the selectors which ruled out the very riders who had come through those tests: most of the riders were professionals. John was the only exception, having jumped both in the bronze medal-winning World Championship team in 1982 and in the silver medal-winning European team in 1983. Michael, with Disney Way, was considered for the World Championships at Dublin after his King George V Gold Cup win at the Royal International, but he did not make the team because of inexperience and doubts about the horse's ability at that level.

Championship team members who had to be left out of Olympic reckoning included David Broome, Harvey Smith, Malcolm Pyrah, Nick Skelton and Liz Edgar. Even looking at the broader picture provided by the computer rankings, the top echelons were mainly professional. In the list published in September 1983, John and Michael Whitaker and Lesley McNaught were the only amateurs in the top ten. Only four others made the top twenty.

The pro-am problem dated back to the early seventies, when there was a move against 'shamateurism', the journalistic name for bogus amateurism. The FEI – the international equestrian federation – under its president, the Duke of Edinburgh, started a movement to make equestrian sport above board as far as amateur status was concerned. The British Show Jumping Association decided to put the sport's house in order in this country with a 'come clean' campaign. Several top riders admitted they were making their living from the sport and, although there were a few protests, most did turn professional. There were a number of advantages, including permission for horses to carry a commercial prefix to their names – the best form of publicity for a sponsor. The purge was supposed to be mirrored in other countries, but it was not, partly because there was not so much commercial sponsorship abroad as in Britain.

In Germany and France a lot of government money was being injected into equestrian sport in order to back the Olympic effort. Show jumping governing bodies in those countries were afraid that making the top riders professional would weaken the Olympic team and, as a result, reduce the amount of government money the sport could attract. Also in those countries several of the best horses were state owned, so the question of commercial backing for them – in return for a company prefix – arose much less than in Britain. These horses were provided by the state for the best riders to use in championships, with the Olympics as the ultimate goal.

Fortunately the mood on the pro-am issue changed in this country and by 1983 competitors of Olympic standard could do most things a professional did without losing their precious amateur status. The one marked restriction remaining was that they could not add commercial prefixes

106

to their horses' names, which was an important factor for some sponsors. The BSJA concentrated its effort on keeping as many competitors as possible amateur and this halting of the professional tide left a number of good riders still eligible for the Games. Also the International Olympic Committee relaxed the rules surrounding the sponsorship of amateurs, although competitors did still have to come up with some job description other than their sport. John and Michael's work alibi was 'farmer'.

Despite these constraints, the chairman of the selectors, General Sir Cecil Blacker, was optimistic about the standard of rider from which the committee could choose. He was sure the pick of the young amateurs would be capable of tackling Olympic courses. The only drawbacks would be that most of them lacked international experience and would have difficulty securing a ride on a horse with the necessary special ability. The short-list announced on 21 October 1983, was of riders only. The idea was to draw attention to the ones with Olympic potential in the hope that efforts would then be concentrated on finding them the best possible horses. It also gave riders like John and Michael, who already had top class horses, a chance to plan their build-up.

The seven riders named on that first list were: John and Michael Whitaker, Lesley McNaught, David Bowen, Steven Smith, Tony Newbery and Gary Gillespie. Later, Scotsman John Brown was added to the list; it was thought that as a skilful lightweight rider he might be an acceptable substitute if one of the other contenders was injured. A more significant addition was Tim Grubb, who was brought up in Leicestershire but moved to the United States in 1981 on marrying American international rider Michelle McEvoy. Tim had been with John in the silver medal-winning team at the 'Substitute Olympics' at Rotterdam in 1980. He also had a horse full of ability called Linky, a Dutch-bred bay bought from Malcolm Pyrah. Tim and Linky impressed at the World Cup final in the spring of 1984, were second in the first US Olympic trial and had

107

many other successes at American shows where courses were likely to be a good warm-up for Los Angeles.

However, back in Britain finding suitable mounts for short-listed riders was to present more difficulty. On paper, John was the one with the least to worry about. Ryan's Son had won £45,612 in the year ending with the 1983 Horse of the Year Show, making him the top international money winner and the leader of the league for combined national and international winnings. He had shown in both the European Championships and the Hickstead Derby that he was still one of the best horses in Europe. John's father had said that Ryan would be just right for the Olympics in Los Angeles, despite his sixteen years, because he was 'soberer in his mind' and more economical in his efforts to clear fences than he had been in his youth.

John felt he would have his best chance of a medal with Ryan. He also knew the horse had cleared the European Championship fences comfortably, so if the Olympic courses were similar they would be within his scope. But his big worry was that they would be considerably tougher, and that would mean putting Ryan through a harrowing test which could finish his career prematurely. He thought about the horse's age and his long and loyal service – 1984 was to be their twelfth season together. Was it fair to reward Ryan with yet another test? His sentimental attachment to the horse and a desire to preserve him at the top for as long as possible were the main negative factors, and both Clare and his mother expressed reservations.

After Ryan's 1983 performances the selectors were very keen to persuade John to take him to Los Angeles. 'If he keeps it up it would be folly to leave him behind for the Olympics,' said General Blacker. A compromise suggestion was that John should take Ryan just for the team event and spare him the slightly harder courses put up for the individual. John was never keen on that idea. If Ryan was fit and on form in the lead-up to the Olympics, he wanted to have two cracks at getting a medal. If the horse was below par, he should not go at all. Time would tell, when Ryan was brought out for the 1984 season, and meanwhile

John hedged his bets by suggesting Saint Mungo as his reserve horse. He asked Mr Brown at the Horse of the Year Show whether he could aim Mungo for the Games and the owner was delighted at the prospect.

The 16.2 h.h. quality chestnut had the ability to jump big fences and cope with long combinations. He had won an international class at the Hickstead Derby meeting and been in the money in the back-up classes at the European Championships. He had a bold, sensible temperament which had helped him progress from Grade B to international classes in one season. The horse would be ten in 1984 and in his prime physically, but his lack of experience was a major drawback. Nevertheless, John felt that if Ryan was not available it would be better for him to ride a horse he knew well than try to scratch together a last-minute partnership with a strange animal.

Michael Whitaker had substantial international winnings on three horses in 1983, Disney Way, Overton Amanda and Courtway. They were fourteenth, fifteenth and sixteenth respectively on the international prize money table. However, he was certain that Amanda was the one for the Olympics because of the ease with which she jumped big fences. Amanda, a dark bay mare, was bred in Cheshire and her Thoroughbred blood showed in her handsome conformation. It was expected that the finer horses would cope better with the heat of Los Angeles than the cobby ones. Amanda had been brought out by Adrian Marsh, who had also trained the young Anglezarke. Michael took over the ride in 1982 when she was eight and just Grade A. She kept improving and her best win in 1983 was the Barcelona Grand Prix, where she was also in the winning Nations Cup team. Michael rode her in five Nations Cups during the season, her first at international level. She never incurred more than 4 faults in a team round. However, she did put in the occasional stop, particularly at water ditches, and she would have to produce a further improvement in 1984 to secure Olympic selection for Michael.

The two least experienced riders on the short-list, Steven Smith, aged twenty-one, and Gary Gillespie, twenty-two, also seemed to have access to horses of outstanding ability. Steven's regular ride, Fairway, was an 18 h.h. Dutch-bred with a powerful jump. It had won a class in Liège, Belgium, on one of the two occasions that Steven had represented Britain in 1983. As soon as Steven was put on the short-list, his father, Harvey, was asked if he would have the chance to try the better known Team Sanyo horses, and he had replied that his younger son could have the pick of the string. It took some months for this promise to materialize, but it was eventually thanks to Harvey and to his elder son, Robert, that Steven got the chance to ride Shining Example. Gary Gillespie had a German-bred chestnut with a huge jump called Goldfink, who was a puissance winner. However, his Olympic challenge in 1984 was made on another impressive horse of German origin, Lorenzo.

Although Lesley McNaught was younger than these two – she was only nineteen when the short-list came out – she had more experience. While a trainee of Ted Edgar, she became Junior European Champion, National Ladies' Champion and was the first woman and the youngest rider to take the Radio Rentals Championship at the Horse of the Year Show. However, she and Ted Edgar fell out in 1983 and she had to go it alone, keeping her best ride, FMS Barbarella.

David Bowen, from Lancashire, had had good results on a succession of horses, including winning the King George V Gold Cup on Scorton. His best horse in 1983 was Coady but, like Barbarella, this mare did not appear to have Olympic potential. Tony Newbery, reserve at the Montreal Olympics, had an even more limited choice of rides.

These were the ones who desperately needed the chance to try out other horses and, once matched up, they would also need time to weld the partnerships. But where were those animals to come from? The main problem was that the best horses in the country tended to be in the hands of the professionals. They needed strings of top horses to land frequent prizes and deliver the necessary publicity for their sponsors and the fact that they had company money behind them made it easier for them to buy class horses. The circle was unlikely to be broken altruistically to give an amateur a chance of an Olympic medal. The professional would at best be giving up part of his living and at worst the horse could be injured or lose its form. To be fair to the professionals, the selectors were no more likely to persuade an amateur, whose riding was not up to championship standard, to lend a brilliant horse. That would mean risking their once-in-a-lifetime chance to succeed at their favourite sport.

Ironically, although the response to the implicit appeal for horses was quite good, the eventual team was basically made up of riders on their usual mounts. However, a lot of water did flow under the bridge in the first part of the 1984 season and the fortunes of David Bowen, Steven Smith, Tony Newbery and Lesley McNaught ebbed and flowed with the form of their horses.

For John there were two main questions: would Ryan be as good in 1984 as in the previous year, and would Saint Mungo show the necessary improvement to be seriously considered as an Olympic horse? The answer to the first came at the World Cup final at Gothenberg, Sweden, where Ryan showed all his usual zest for competition, jumping two clears in the second leg, with a clear and 4 faults in the final leg. Unfortunately John's chance of a good placing had already gone in the first round, a speed class which Clonee Temple had looked like winning, until she stopped at the last two fences. After that John was content to ease Ryan off until the Hickstead international in early June, which gave him several weeks to concentrate on Saint Mungo.

In May all the short-listed riders, except for John Brown and Tim Grubb, went to Spain to compete at three international shows. The idea was to give them practice over continental-style courses, with wider spreads and long combinations, and to weld them into a team. Both General Blacker and team manager Ronnie Massarella are great believers in team spirit, and felt the get-together out of the limelight would increase the riders' support for one another and boost morale. They would also be able to make full use

111

of the advice offered by Peter Robeson, Olympic bronze medallist in 1964, who had been picked as team coach. For those who would have to pick the L.A. team it would be a useful trial of the riders' temperaments as well as of their riding ability.

As well as Saint Mungo, John took his former Foxhunter champion, Hopscotch, and a new ride, Manolito, who had come from Paul Schockemöhle in an exchange deal. It was a good opportunity to put in plenty of training on these horses at show grounds with excellent facilities. At Madrid there were three massive collecting rings, with every type of fence to practise over. Mungo was placed in several classes, including the Grand Prix at Jerez de la Frontera. However, he most impressed the selectors by jumping a clear and a 4-fault round in the Nations Cup at Barcelona, the last show on the tour. This was the best score in an otherwise disappointing team performance, which left Britain eighth out of twelve.

Hopscotch was in fine form at Barcelona. He won an early class and, when Saint Mungo was a bit tired after the Nations Cup, John decided to take the younger chestnut in his first Grand Prix. He won it in a timed jump-off, after being one of only two among sixty-four starters to jump a double clear.

The Nations Cup marked an important breakthrough for John, who had always relied on Ryan's Son as his main international ride. It was the first time he had jumped in a British team on another horse. Earlier in the year he had made a similar breakthrough in Grand Prix, when he won these premier events on Clonee Temple at both Antwerp and Dortmund international shows.

Michael Whitaker had a highly successful Spanish trip, winning seven classes on his brilliant speed horse Courtway, but he had left his prospective Olympic mounts, Overton Amanda and Red Flight, at home. He said it was too early in Amanda's campaign to take her so far for such a testing run of shows. Red Flight, the little bay mare on whom he held the world bareback high jump record at 7 feet, had only just returned from a continental trip before the departure for Spain. He still made the Barcelona Nations Cup team, on Tamara, and did well to jump one clear round.

Of the other riders, David Bowen emerged as the best Olympic prospect during the tour, except for a bad round on Brindle Boy in the Nations Cup, which raised questions about the horse's temperament. He had ridden the grey as a novice, and in the winter of 1983–4 had bought him back from Malcolm Bowey, who had had several successes on him from his Northumberland base. Brindle Boy then joined Tony Elliott's string, which David Bowen had taken over from Lionel Dunning early in 1984. Among these the best Olympic prospect was a German-bred chestnut, Boysie, who was fourth in the 1983 national money winning table. David also tried Mr Ross in Spain, but the horse knocked himself in Jerez and had to miss Madrid.

Gary Gillespie also did well enough to gain a Nations Cup place in Barcelona, but two poor rounds showed up his inexperience and greatly diminished his Olympic chances. One rider who impressed the chairman of the selectors, General Blacker, in Spain was Tony Newbery, who was improving all the time on Ryan's Mill, a horse he had acquired for the season from West country rider Claire Rushworth.

In the doldrums were Lesley McNaught and Steven Smith. Lesley's best horse from previous seasons, FMS Barbarella, had needed stitches in a head cut after an accident in one of the frequent downpours. With Tony Elliott's Ona Promise, ridden before by Pam Dunning, she never found form. While Ronnie Massarella was considering whom to put in the Nations Cup team, Ona Promise put in a stop with Lesley which threw her off. Bad luck had struck Steven Smith just before the tour when Fairway went lame and he had had to muddle through with two lesser animals.

After the Spanish trip John said it was the same old story with Britain's Olympic prospects: 'We have good riders, but we don't have the horses.' However, he made a pretty good prediction about the eventual team; himself, Michael, Tim Grubb and David Bowen. Although four weeks on the conti-

113

nent had meant missing several good British shows, John had enjoyed the trip and felt it had done no harm to rest some of the horses left behind – Alan had of course continued with *his* show programme. Ironically the weather had been very wet in Spain, but in Britain there was a drought and John was also glad he had not been pounding his horses over hard ground.

Back in Britain the Olympic hopefuls' first major test was an international meeting at Hickstead on the first weekend in June. This time John's number one horse was Ryan and he jumped superbly in the Grand Prix to land second prize behind Nick Skelton on St James. He was only beaten on time over a galloping course. That performance made John and Ryan virtual certainties for Los Angeles and by then John had talked himself into a positive approach to taking Ryan to the Games.

First of all he had taken seriously the argument that the Olympic courses would not be as bad as some people feared. He was beginning to realize that a good deal of the head shaking was being done by professionals who were ineligible for the Games and, therefore, tended to decry them. He knew the rules were the same as for other championships, and that the maximum width had been reduced after complaints about dangerously large obstacles at the World Championships in Dublin. There was also a view that the Olympic courses would have to be sensible to avoid mayhem among less experienced teams from nations such as Mexico, Japan and Chile. Since Montreal it had been decided to hold the team competition before the more testing individual event, which gave the horses a more logical build-up. John had ridden Bert de Nemethy's courses before and knew that he could get results by testing the rider with tricky distances and tight turns, rather than by flooring the horses over huge fences. He expected clever courses, which would suit the skilful British riders, rather than dangerous ones.

The question of who would join John at Los Angeles was still a burning issue and pessimists were saying that, whoever was chosen, the team would stand little chance.

David Bowen boosted his hopes by winning an international class at Hickstead, but Michael slightly irritated the selectors by not jumping Overton Amanda in the Grand Prix. He had only just started her in serious competitions after returning from Spain and he felt that, at that stage, the Hickstead water ditches were too big to put her at without more practice. He knew she could take a dislike to this type of fence and felt it would be tempting fate to throw her in at the deep end. He wisely stayed at Hickstead after the show was over and put in some useful training over the double of ditches.

Steven Smith had brought Fairway back into competition, but the horse was clearly lacking match fitness. So the question was again put to Harvey: 'When are you going to let him try one of your top horses?' The hottest property in the Team Sanyo at that time was Shining Example, known as Norman – a Dutch-bred horse whom Harvey had taught to do 'Barbara Woodhouse-style' tricks. He had clocked up wins at home and abroad with Harvey and Robert in May, including one of the Hickstead classes with Robert. After that show both Robert and Harvey agreed to stand aside to let Steven have a go on the twelve-year-old chestnut and he immediately capitalised with a win at the Royal Cornwall. Meanwhile, Lesley McNaught's last hope, Mr Ross, whom she started to ride at Hickstead, still did not help her back to winning form.

Tony Newbery's luck was also out. At first there were doubts about whether the Rushworths were willing for Ryan's Mill to go to the Olympics. Then Ronnie Massarella secured their acquiescence, but it was to no avail because Ryan's Mill suffered a slight injury and was not sound enough to be considered for the most crucial test, the Aachen International Show. The rest of the short-listed riders, barring John Brown and Tim Grubb, made the trip to West Germany. The Aachen courses are renowned for their toughness and the British riders would face competition from Olympic probables from ten countries.

Following the same principle as in 1983, John decided not to take Ryan because it would not have suited the

115

horse's Olympic build-up to produce peak performances five weeks before departing for Los Angeles. John was also still intent on proving Saint Mungo's worth as a back-up horse, so that if anything went wrong with Ryan he would still stand a good chance of being in the team. Mungo had improved every week since being thrown in at the deep end by going to Spain after only a few spring shows. Back in Britain he had won a couple of area international trials – and it was little more than a year since he had reached Grade A.

John's faith in Mungo was justified by his opening performance at Aachen, when he won a major class. Michael, who also had a point to prove on Overton Amanda, finished third and that was just the start of his hammering home his case for selection. The next day he won the German International Championship, when he was easily the fastest of the three horses to go clear in the jump-off. In his wake were World Champion Norbert Koof and European Champion Paul Schockemöhle. Britain's morale was further boosted before the Nations Cup with wins in relay competitions by Michael, David Bowen and Steven Smith.

John and Michael Whitaker, David Bowen and Steven Smith made up the team for the Nations Cup – effectively Europe's dress rehearsal for the Olympics. They covered themselves in glory by finishing second to the Swiss, the European Champions, and there was only one fence in it. The Swiss finished with a zero score, Britain with 4 faults and France had a total of 12 to finish third of the fourteen teams. Michael Whitaker, on Amanda, and David Bowen, on Boysie, jumped double clears, and Steven Smith had 4 faults in each round. He was particularly unlucky in the second round as a fence fell after a mere tap by Shining Example, whereas when one of the Swiss horses clouted it, it stayed up. John, who rode last, had to repeat his first-round clear to secure a jump-off with the Swiss. But Mungo showed his inexperience when photographers distracted him at a parallel, which he had down. Typically John also partly blamed himself for the lapse. 'He had jumped the

fence before extra well. I relaxed slightly and he got a bit
long. When he peeped at the photographers I lost him.'
Mungo was also in the water, but that had no bearing on
the final team score.

The Nations Cup performance caused a lot of word-eating
among those who had written off Britain's amateur team.
At last stories appeared giving them a chance of winning
a medal – although the optimism soon faded.

After Aachen John was left with mixed feelings about
Saint Mungo. The horse had exceeded expectations by
winning a class and by going so well in the Nations Cup,
but in two other competitions he had put in a stop, and
John was aware that he was becoming a bit fed up with
continually jumping big fences. He had always said that
the Olympics had come a year too early for Mungo because
of his lack of experience. But the horse was mature and
bold, so an extraordinary improvement had seemed
possible.

He did come on well enough to justify completely his
inclusion in the LA team as a reserve horse, but he could
not be seriously considered as an alternative to a fit Ryan.
After Aachen Mungo went through a slightly lacklustre
period, which confirmed that he had been asked to do a bit
too much too soon. John described it as a setback which he
was confident Mungo would soon get over.

Michael's performance at Aachen had squashed doubts
about Amanda's Olympic potential. She did not have a
single fence down at the show, which she rounded off in
style with a third in the Grand Prix. As well as coping
comfortably with the size of the fences, she had also jumped
water ditches without batting an eyelid – her post-
Hickstead training appeared to have done the trick.

Before Hickstead there had been one or two fears that
Michael would end up out in the cold for the Olympics, like
John in 1976. He had started the season a firm favourite
for selection because of his riding ability, experience and
the fact that Amanda undoubtedly had plenty of scope. He
also had a winning temperament – he had landed a coveted
title virtually every year since he won the Leading Junior

Jumper of the Year championship at Wembley in 1976. However, because he did not take Amanda to Spain or jump her in the Hickstead Grand Prix, the selectors became a little restive and wondered whether the mare's form was good enough – 1984 was, after all, only her second year at international level. However, only John and Tim Grubb had enjoyed copybook preparation of their Olympic horses early in the season, so Michael was never seriously in danger of being excluded from the five-rider squad.

After Aachen, with Tim Grubb going well in the United States and Tony Newbery's ride Ryan's Mill returning to fitness, the selectors suddenly had a problem deciding whom to leave out. Their last chance to review form came at the Royal Show in the first week of July. The only complication was that David Bowen's ride, Boysie, was unable to jump after injuring his side. The wound was just where the girth went, preventing him wearing a saddle until it had healed.

David Bowen showed the strength in depth of Tony Elliott's string by riding San Francisco to equal first place with Michael Whitaker in the first big class. John had a win with Ryan on the second day and Michael landed the National Championship with Overton Amanda hours before the selectors met to make their final decision.

With John, Michael and David in good form – which was being mirrored by Tim Grubb across the Atlantic – the crucial question was whether the fifth rider would be Steven Smith or Tony Newbery. Although Tony had jumped two clears in the National Championship, taking fourth prize, his form at the Royal had not been good enough to make up for missing Aachen. Steven had continued to jump consistently well on Shining Example, who was a more experienced horse than Ryan's Mill. Steven had kept his cool through every test of temperament and it was a great achievement for him to form so good a relationship with Shining Example in so few weeks. He knew Aachen had been a turning point in his chances, after Fairway's lameness had deprived him of a serious challenge in Spain. It was on the earlier tour, particularly in the Barcelona Grand

Prix, that Tony had impressed. But Spain could not be compared with Aachen, so Steven got the decision after long discussion by the selectors.

The team picked for the Olympics was:

John Whitaker, who would be twenty-nine during the Games, with Ryan's Son and Saint Mungo. He was also named as team captain.

Michael Whitaker, twenty-four, who, with his wife Veronique, also a show jumper and formerly a Belgian international, ran a yard at Stockport, Cheshire. His horse for the Games was Overton Amanda.

David Bowen, thirty-four, a father of two from Preston, Lancashire, former winner of the King George V Gold Cup and long respected by his fellow show jumpers for his riding skill – and as a nice guy.

Steven Smith, twenty-one, Harvey's younger son, from Bingley, West Yorkshire. He had had an early taste of international success in two gold medal-winning Junior European Championship teams. His ride would be the Team Sanyo's Shining Example.

Tim Grubb, thirty-one, had been with John in the silver medal team at the Substitute Olympics in Rotterdam in 1980, before he married and moved out to the United States. He was well remembered by the rest of the team from his years in Leicestershire.

The four riders based in Britain had one international outing at Hickstead before their departure for LA. They had a strange start to the meeting after dashing down from the Great Yorkshire Show at Harrogate only to scatter a few poles in the first major competition. Team manager Ronnie Massarella gave headline writers a field day by accusing them of riding like 'a bunch of fairies'. Only John escaped some of the well-meant wrath by jumping clear on Ryan – but with time faults!

It was the signal for the dirge to restart about the amateur team's lack of a chance at the Games. With Nick Skelton, Malcolm Pyrah and Liz Edgar all on good form, conservative onlookers would have rewritten history to undo Britain's move to make the top riders of the 1970s

119

professionals. The moaners got the upper hand when the team of four Olympic riders could only finish fourth out of five in the Nations Cup, beaten by West Germany, France and Australia – whose riders were responding well to training by Ted Edgar. John on Ryan and David Bowen on Boysie both did creditably, each jumping a clear and a 4-fault round. Michael and Steven each had rounds of 4 and 8 on their Olympic mounts.

In fact, none of the rounds were bad and the British were only three fences behind the victorious Germans. In writing off the performance, many commentators ignored a series of positive signs. Ryan's Son, who had had a very easy season to save him for LA, hit only one fence in five rounds at the Hickstead meeting to show that his build-up was well on course. Overton Amanda had yet to produce her best form at Hickstead, and after jumping about twenty clears in a row in late June/early July, she would benefit from a couple of weeks' rest from competition before facing the Olympic test. Steven Smith rode especially well in the second round of the Nations Cup, showing just the sort of determination that would be needed in the Olympics. His horse, Shining Example, would also benefit from the rest. David Bowen's Boysie had just returned to the ring after a lay off of nearly three weeks caused by injury, and in LA the team would be strengthened by Tim Grubb.

John said it was an advantage that the team were not going to LA as favourites, because it lessened the pressure. All the disparaging comments only served to make the riders more determined to prove the pessimists wrong. He always believed the team had a chance because it was a one-off competition in which a crucial factor would be whether riders cracked. In Nations Cups and the international championships it was surprising how many made mistakes. John had great faith in the riding ability of his fellow team members and, since seeing the horses go so well in Aachen, he knew this would be no team of outsiders. His misgivings about taking Ryan had been replaced by enthusiasm at the chance to compete.

This was fed by people coming up to slap him on the back

and wish him luck, and at Ryan's final outing before the flight he had a standing ovation. It was a comparatively small show at Nostell Priory, near Wakefield, and the commentator had been rather quiet all day. However, when he invited the crowd to wish John all the best for LA, everyone leapt to their feet and cheered. Ryan jumped two clears in the £100 open, but his scores did not count because John had already ridden the maximum number of three Grade As in the class. He had been doing even more riding than usual in the preceding three weeks because his assistant, Alan Fazakerley, had cracked a couple of ribs and been badly shaken and bruised when dragged by a horse at a Doncaster show. With the grit typical of show jumpers, Alan was determined to be back in the saddle while John was away.

10

The Great Test

Show jumping was first staged at the Olympics in 1912. Before that the only similar competitions for horses – held at the Paris Games in 1900 – had been prize jumping, high jump and long jump. It took Britain until 1948 in London to win her first show jumping medal, although her polo teams had carried off a fistful of medals and the three-day event team had won its first medal, a bronze, at Berlin, in 1936. The Second World War put a stop to two sets of Games, due in 1940 and 1944, and when they restarted in London, in 1948, the show jumpers began a formidable run of success. It was twenty-eight years and seven more Olympics before they came home empty handed. The team which set the ball rolling, with a bronze medal, comprised Harry Llewellyn on Foxhunter, Henry Nicoll with Kilgeddin and Arthur Carr with Monty. All the riders had an army background.

In Helsinki, in 1952, Harry Llewellyn and Foxhunter were again at the heart of the team, with Wilf White on Nizefela – famous for kicking back over fences – and Douggie Stewart on Aherlow. This trio won Britain's only gold medal for show jumping, beating Chile and the United States into the silver and bronze medal positions. Wilf White was very unlucky not to win the individual gold, too. In the second round Nizefela jumped the water but landed in a puddle beyond the tape. His rider has always been convinced that the judge mistook the splash for a fault at the obstacle. He finished the round with just 4 faults, when a clear would have clinched the gold. Four years later Wilf White and Nizefela were again in the team, which this time won a bronze medal. His compatriots were Pat Smythe on Flanagan, the first woman to jump at the Olympics, and Peter Robeson on Scorchin. That was the last team Olympic medal Britain won at the sport – until 1984.

However, individual riders had kept the flag flying. David Broome won bronze medals in 1960, at Rome, with Sunsalve, and in 1968, at Mexico, with Mister Softee. In between, at Tokyo, Peter Robeson won a bronze on Firecrest. The best individual performances have come from women riders. In 1968 Marion Coakes (now Mould) went one better than David Broome to take the silver on her pony, Stroller, the smallest animal in the competition. In 1972, at Munich, it was Ann Moore's turn on Psalm, to win silver.

In nine Olympic Games, up to and including the substitute event in 1980, British show jumpers had only once come home without a medal. That was at Montreal in 1976 and even then Debbie Johnsey came within a whisker of the rostrum by finishing fourth after a jump-off. The three-day eventers also had a fine record, winning the team gold in 1956, 1968 and 1972. At Munich, in 1972, Richard Meade made it a double by winning the individual gold on Laurieston – he remains the only British rider to gain that Olympic honour. Other individual eventing medals came from Frank Weldon, bronze in 1956, and Derek Allhusen, silver in 1968. However, British riders had never won an Olympic medal at dressage.

The show jumpers who flew out to Los Angeles on 26 July 1984, were aiming to become the first British team to win an Olympic medal since 1956 and they were far more confident about their chances than most observers. The youngest member, Steven Smith, said in a newspaper interview before his departure that everyone was being 'a bit silly' about the team's prospects. 'There are a lot of teams where things can go wrong and I can't see anything going wrong with ours.' He stuck his neck out and said he would be very surprised if they returned without a medal.

The four British-based riders, John and Michael Whitaker, Steven Smith and David Bowen, team manager Ronnie Massarella and coach Peter Robeson were joined in

123

the Olympic village by Tim Grubb. The seven of them shared chalet-style quarters on the University of California Los Angeles campus, situated in a salubrious western suburb of the city, which has a population of 3.5 million. They had three days to get their bearings before the horses arrived and they soon discovered that the village had just about every form of entertainment they could wish for, from games rooms and swimming pools to cinemas and discos. They had a mini bus to help them get about the sprawling city.

It was about thirty-five miles to Santa Anita racecourse, where the show jumping events would be held and the horses stabled. To get there they travelled through Beverley Hills and Hollywood, and headed north-east on to the 210 Foothill Freeway, past Passadena to Arcadia. The racecourse was set in blissful suburbia, where the houses were spacious and the gardens lush. Although it had not rained since Christmas, sprinklers were used everywhere, even on the roadside. On a clear day it was a perfect mixture of blue skies, green grass and palm trees. In the background were the San Gabriel mountains and their stubbly slopes gave a truer reflection of the hot, dry climate. Daytime temperatures varied from 80° to 100°F. like a mediterranean island. The only drawback was the smog, which wafted inland from the city traffic and came to rest against the mountains. On a bad day it would obliterate them, even though the foothills were little more than a mile away. On a good day a breeze would disperse the fume cloud before it reached Santa Anita, leaving a holiday brochure backdrop

Before the horses arrived the riders had a taste of what the Olympic movement was all about, at the opening ceremony on 28 July. They marched into the Coliseum with the other British athletes behind three-day eventer Lucinda Green, who had been chosen to carry the flag. They joined in the celebration of international harmony and the spirit of sportsmanship, backed by a Hollywood-style musical show The audience of about 90,000 set a record for participation by lifting up coloured segments to create a giant mosaic of national flags. When they watched the Olympic flame fly round the Olympic rings and up to the great torch above the stadium, our riders knew the county show circuit would never seem the same again.

The next day the seven horses flew in, minus Tony Elliott's San Francisco, who was to have been one of David Bowen's reserves. The bay horse was lame but, at that stage, it looked as though David still had a good hand without him in Boysie and Brindle Boy. The horses were transported in crates, which were padded and partitioned like two-horse trailers without roofs or wheels. The crates were hoisted on and off the plane with forklift machines and they could be moved up and down the fuselage on rollers. Travelling with the horses were the grooms – Angie Padfield went with John's two – and professionals who specialized in the transport of animals by air. The worst moments for the horses are take-off and landing, so the pilot makes these manoeuvres less steep than he would for humans and as smooth as possible.

As soon as the horses arrived at Santa Anita they were quarantined for two days. They could be walked out within the quarantine station, but the enforced inactivity was not the ideal routine for super-fit horses. In the regular stable area the boxes were in barns, either side of a central aisle. Each horse had its own air conditioning fan, and sprinklers sent a continual stream of water over the roofs to keep the stables cool. To avoid upsetting the horses' diet the team had brought over food from England, including vitamin and mineral supplements and Horsehage, which John had introduced to Ryan and Mungo's diet three weeks before their departure. This cut-grass bulk food is a dust-free and nutritious alternative to hay.

The horses restarted work on Wednesday, 1 August, three days before the 'friendly' practice competition. To avoid the worst of the heat and the possible midday smog, the riders began exercise soon after 6a.m., which meant getting up at 4.30a.m. because it was an hour's drive to the racecourse from the village. It was four hours earlier than John's usual rising time! The horses did not seem to suffer from jet lag. John felt this was because their lives have less of a routine than those of humans, they sleep and – to some extent – eat when they want to, rather than obeying a clock.

John tried to keep Ryan's exercise routine the same as it would have been at home. He took advantage of the scores of acres of grass gallops and sand paddocks to give him the miles of trotting and cantering work he would normally have had over the Yorkshire hills. He knew that too much schooling and practice jumping would excite Ryan and make him more difficult to handle. He took him over a course of fences in one of the six fully-equipped practice rings, but what the headstrong sixteen-year-old could really have done with was a couple of serious competitions to concentrate his mind. It was just as well John also had Saint Mungo to work on so that he was not tempted to do too much with Ryan, which would only have wound him up.

For the rest of the day the team stuck together for sightseeing, sunbathing or socialising under the watchful eye of Ronnie Massarella, who was a father figure and nurse maid rolled into one. A pleasant duty was to support the three-day event team on its way to a silver medal – and Virginia Holgate landing the bonus of a bronze in the individual championship. The cross-country took them 110 miles south of Los Angeles, down Freeway 5 which partly follows the Pacific coast, to Fairbanks ranch, near San Diego. The former residence of Douglas Fairbanks had been converted into an undulating and grassy cross-country course on its way to becoming a luxury golf club. Getting the course ready for the eventers involved an earth-moving marathon as well as months of work building a picturesque set of fences. Most reminiscent of the ranch's Hollywood connections was a combination through a Wild West ghost town. Another obstacle was modelled on the rattle snakes which used to infest the area; by the time 50,000 spectators had arrived, the reptiles had cleared out.

The eventers, who had suffered some harsh dressage marks, pulled up from fourth to second that day, less than two fences behind the United States. After a rest day they arrived back at Santa Anita for the show jumping, on 3 August, and pulled up to a mere 3.2 faults behind the home team. Their success boosted morale for the whole equestrian camp.

Another massive earth-moving operation had been mounted at Santa Anita itself to build the show jumping arena. It was like a giant sand pit, with retaining walls ranging from 18 inches to 7 feet, to give a level sand-and-soil stage bridging the racetrack. The arena measured about 70 by 200 yards and three temporary stands had been constructed across the racecourse and opposite the permanent grandstand to provide 34,000 seats.

Before the practice competition there was one worry in the show jumping camp – Boysie's health. The horse would look all right as he came out of the stable, but would develop muscular stiffness in his back and hindquarters when he started work. At one stage his muscles started to quiver. Some of the symptoms were similar to azoturia, a muscle problem which can afflict a horse in hard condition after a period of enforced idleness. Ronnie Massarella said something in the horse's food or water could be disagreeing with him and affecting his kidneys, although he was getting the same as the others and there was no reason to suspect any foul play. Boysie was not lame, just stiff, and although he was improving the main problem was that he could not be worked properly.

On the morning of the practice competition, Saturday, 4 August, there was much discussion about whether Boysie would jump, but he was eventually ruled not sound enough. This was a blow for David Bowen, who had already suffered bad luck with San Francisco. Just as disappointed was the owner, Tony Elliott, who had made four horses available for Olympic consideration during the year, and who was now seeing the best ones fall by the wayside. His frustration was compounded by restrictions at Santa Anita which did not allow owners to visit their horses as they wished. They were confined to one visiting hour a day and the stipulated time varied and was often inconvenient.

The warm-up course lived up to its name, with just one upright at 5 feet 3 inches and the rest of the fences varying from 4 feet 6 inches to 5 feet. Many clears were jumped, but the time was so tight that faults were common, ¼ fault being incurred for each second over the time allowed. The only British rider to jump clear inside the time and earn a souvenir prize was Tim Grubb on Linky. John had just 4 faults on Mungo, at a spread over water in the combination. Mr and Mrs Brown, watching in the stands, were delighted at the horse's performance in such awe-inspiring circumstances – a huge crowd had turned up even though there were no medals to be won. Michael looked as though he was going to jump clear – until Amanda hit the last.

Ryan, who had not been in a competition for two weeks, skipped about like a four-year-old, making things difficult for John. He had two fences down and John had to slow him right down to get him to concentrate, which meant 3 time faults. He said afterwards it was what he expected, because the horse was so fresh. But he had let Ryan know he was misbehaving and made him listen over the second half of the course. Steven Smith kept up his consistent record on Shining Example with just one down. But David Bowen diminished his chances of consideration for the team with Brindle Boy by making a mistake going into the combination; one fence fell and the horse had to stop, incurring 7 faults – plus more for exceeding the time. It looked as though his only chance of being in the team would be if Boysie rapidly regained 100 per cent fitness to enable him to have a proper workout before the championship three days later. It was unlikely he would make it.

Ronnie Massarella picked the team on Monday, 6 August, the day before the team competition. David Bowen was left out because, although Boysie had passed a vet's inspection, he had not had the necessary work. 'It would not be fair to put him in at the deep end,' said Mr Massarella. So the team was John and Michael Whitaker, Tim Grubb and Steven Smith.

Michael, on Overton Amanda, would go first. Mr Massarella said he could be relied on not to flap and would glean plenty of information about the course to pass on to the second rider, Steven Smith, the least experienced. Steven would be able to see how others tackled the course, 'But he won't have long to dwell on things,' said the team boss. Tim Grubb would go third. He had plenty of experience and a super horse; a good round from him would take some of the pressure off the last to go. John was 'the obvious choice' for that position because, whatever happened, he would not panic.

After a week of comparative relaxation, tension hit the riders as the day dawned for the team competition. Not a word was spoken as they travelled to Santa Anita in their mini bus. Plenty of cigarettes were smoked and Steven Smith bit down the fingernails he had been growing. The riders felt a bit better when they saw the course: it was at least jumpable, and as they walked it the feeling grew that it would suit them. As expected, Bert de Nemethy had chosen to set rider problems rather than 'kill' the horses. The cups were shallow, which would benefit the careful jumpers and avoid hurting the horses who hit fences.

The half-mile course started over a staggered spread, with a 4 foot 9 inch back pole and a spread of 4 feet 11 inches. The rider then had to do a tight U-turn, under the noses of the spectators, to a 4 foot 11 inch-upright. A 90° left hand turn gave only a short run to number three, a true parallel of planks, with a 6 foot 3 inch spread. The biggest fence on the course came next, a triple bar, with a 5 foot 3 inch back rail and a spread of nearly 7 feet. Then the course followed an S-shape at the top end of the arena, over two picturesque uprights – a Japanese Gate at 5 feet 3 inches and a Sail Boat – and two spreads over water ditches, with criss-crossed poles. There were tricky distances between the next three, a gate followed by 15 feet of water followed by a 6 foot 3 inch-wide true parallel. Most riders pressed on for long strides to the water and then had to apply the brakes to re-adjust the stride length before the parallel.

Then came the obstacle which caused the most grief, a combination of three spreads in a dull red colour similar to the sandy loam surface of the arena. The true parallel going in was 4 feet 9 inches high, then there was one long stride to a triple bar 5 feet 1 inch high and 6 feet 7 inches wide,

15 Obstacles
Speed: 400 m. per min.
Length of course: __790m__
Time allowed: __119 secs__
Time limit: __238 secs__

GAMES OF THE XXIIIRD OLYMPIAD
TEAM JUMPING COMPETITION
Tuesday August 7, 1984
10:00 h.

Jump off:
No. 1–2–11–12ABC–14A–15
Speed: 400 m. per min.
Length of course: __420m__
Time allowed: __63 secs__
Time limit: __126 secs__
Number 14B will be removed

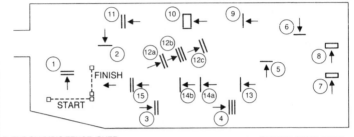

1 THE OLYMPIC FENCE: OXER

Ht. Front 1.40   Ht. Rear 1.45
Spread 1.50

2. STAR IN MOTION

Ht. Front 1.50

3 ROYAL BLUE: OXER

Ht. Front 1.45   Ht. Rear 1.45
Spread 1.90

4 BEVERLY HILLS FENCE:
TRIPLE BAR

Ht. Front 1.00   Ht. Mid. 1.37
Ht. Rear 1.60   Spread 2.10

5 JAPANESE GATE

Ht. Front 1.60

6 SAIL BOAT

Ht. Front 1.55

7 GARDEN GATE: OXER

Ht. Front 1.45   Ht. Rear 1.45
Spread 1.80

8 GARDEN PILLARS: OXER

Ht. Front 1.45   Ht. Rear 1.45
Spread 1.80

9 WESTLAKE IRON GATE

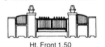

Ht. Front 1.50

10 WATER JUMP

Spread 4.60

11 RAIN FOREST: OXER

Ht. Front 1.50   Ht. Rear 1.50
Spread 1.90

12a CALIFORNIA RED WOOD:
OXER

Ht. Front 1.45   Ht. Rear 1.45
Spread 1.80

12b CALIFORNIA RED WOOD:
TRIPLE BAR

Ht. Front 1.00   Ht. Mid. 1.30
Ht. Rear 1.55   Spread 2.00

12c·CALIFORNIA RED WOOD:
OXER

Ht. Front 1.50   Ht. Rear 1.50
Spread 1.80

13 CARACAS PINK WALL

Ht. Front 1.60

14a GLADSTONE GATE

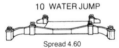

Ht. Front 1.55

14b GLADSTONE GATE

Ht. Front 1.55

15 MEXICAN. OXER

Ht. Front 1.50   Ht. Rear 1.50
Spread 2.00

Measurements in metres

130

followed by two more long strides to another true parallel at 4 feet 11 inches high. After well and truly opening up the horses, de Nemethy then set a tricky line of uprights for the final run down the centre of the arena towards home. First came a 5 foot 3 inch-wall, then an irregular distance to a very short two-striding double of dark green gates. Fence fifteen, the last, was a true parallel, with a 6 foot 7 inch-spread. The time allowed was 119 seconds. Thankfully it was not as tight as for the practice competition.

Fifteen countries had entered teams of four for the event and Ronnie Massarella rightly predicted that Britain's main rivals would be the United States, West Germany, Switzerland, Canada, France and Spain. The Germans were drawn first, followed by four less threatening nations: Italy, Australia, Belgium and Japan, then three hot rivals came together: Switzerland, Canada and the United States. The Europeans could relax for a few minutes while Mexico and Chile went ninth and tenth, then came France, with Britain drawn twelfth. The only serious team behind Britain was Spain, drawn last, after Argentina and Brazil.

The first competitor to go, Fritz Ligges on a typically powerful German horse, showed just how formidable the combination of spreads was by breaking one of the back poles. Harvey Smith had said this was the only place where horses would come down – none did, but the California Red Woods, as the three elements were known, took quite a battering. The first rider to clear them was the eighth-to-go, Joe Fargis, on the aptly named bay Thoroughbred mare, Touch of Class. He went on to complete the first clear round. When Michael came in there were no horses on 4 faults and only one on 8. Amanda had down the first of the two ditches and the spread after the water; she sailed through the combination and finished with 8 faults. After the first set of fifteen riders had gone, Britain was equal second with Canada behind the United States.

The next set produced another clear, Swiss rider Heidi Robbiani on Jessica – an Irish-bred chestnut mare who was so hot a property a story had circulated the previous winter that an American had bought her for a huge sum. Fortunately for Ms Robbiani, one of only three women in the competition, the deal did not materialize. Lesley Burr, for the United States, just had down the last on Albany to consolidate the home team's flying start.

Steven Smith cleared the first few fences, but Shining Example looked a bit too sharp and had down the second of the ditch fences after veering off a straight line. He refused at the next, but Steven wasted no time getting him over, and then recovered well. He had down one part of the combination and was a bit unlucky that both parts of the double of uprights fell, for a total of 19 faults. He was disappointed and said the horse had jumped better than his score suggested.

The first rider to fall off was the third Italian, Filippo Moyersoen. He was going well, with just one of the first ten fences down, when suddenly, between the water and the parallel, his horse swerved violently. Both rider and saddle had slid sideways. The leather girth had broken, so his efforts to refix the saddle were in vain and he was eliminated.

By the time Tim Grubb went, the forty-second to go, there were still only two clear rounds and only one with 4 faults, two had been eliminated and a Mexican had completed the course with 46½ faults. Tim gave Britain just the boost that was needed with a clear round: Linky made little of the fences and Tim's experience over United States courses showed. He pulled Britain back into third place behind the United States and Switzerland. All that was needed was a good round from John and Ryan, to enable Steven's score to be discarded, to secure second place at the halfway stage and to set up a challenge to the Americans.

It was about 2 p.m., smog had obliterated the mountains and the intense heat led to frequent pleas from the announcer for people to cover their heads, seek shade and drink plenty. Ryan appeared unaffected during the warm-up; if anything he was too fresh. In the small collecting ring attached to the arena entrance John was giving him a final jump when he felt the horse lose his footing. Ryan did not mind what sort of going he jumped on – from mud to ground like concrete – but he did mind when the Santa Anita soil went from under him. John gave him a couple more jumps to try to settle him and he only had a short breather before going in.

From the start Ryan was not at his best and kept tapping poles. John kept him clear until fence eleven; then one part of the combination and both parts of the double also fell. John partly blamed himself for concentrating too much on accuracy at the expense of rhythm and sending Ryan forward. His total of 16 did count towards Britain's first round total of 24, but it left the team equal fourth with Switzerland and Canada. The United States led with just 4 faults, Melanie Smith on Calypso having jumped one of only four clears in the first round. Lying second was West Germany with 20 faults, and Spain was third with 21.5.

At first John thought he had blown it. He had expected to do a round of 8 faults or less to give Britain a comfortable hold on the silver. He could not remember when Ryan had last had as many as 16 faults. It was time for the team to rally round and a bit of clear thinking soon told them they still had a good medal chance. Although the Americans had got away, the next five teams were within one fence of each other and France, on 25¾ faults, was also within one fence of the three sharing fourth place. The fight for the silver and bronze was wide open as the twelve best teams went into the second round. Belgium, Chile and Argentina were out and Mexico later withdrew.

David Bowen and Peter Robeson showed that you don't have to be in the saddle to play an important part in a team contest. They had already consoled Steven after his 19-fault round, bolstering his confidence for a much better effort second time, when John came out of the ring equally despondent. The three of them racked their brains to find reasons for Ryan's uncharacteristic performance and to decide what to change for the second round. They agreed that John should jump without spurs, avoid the small collecting ring, where Ryan had slipped, and that the horse should have more flat work and less jumping to get him to concentrate.

John had more than two hours to wait before he jumped again. Meanwhile Michael got the team off to a cracking start with a clear, Amanda being one of three horses to finish on a total of 8, a score only bettered by Touch of Class, who had a double clear, and Jessica, who had a refusal and 2 time faults in the second round for a total of 5. Steven Smith rode with great coolness and determination for 8 faults and, with the first two riders from Germany, Switzerland, Canada, France and Spain having worse combined totals than Britain, the silver was within their grasp. If Tim Grubb could repeat his first round clear it would be won without John having to jump again – and he admitted part of him hoped that would happen. When Conrad Homfeld jumped a clear round for the United States it gave them a grand total of 12 faults and they had won without Melanie Smith having to jump again.

Unfortunately, the American announcer chose to broadcast the inevitable victory just as Tim Grubb was entering the tunnel for his second round. The hullaballoo of patriotic cheering upset Linky. 'I was on a different horse after that,' said Tim. He knocked down an early fence, six more poles hit the dust and he was a second over the time allowed for a total of 28¼ faults.

By the time Tim was half way round, John had put on his hat and left the ringside to start working Ryan. As the last set of riders got ready to jump, Britain was lying sixth. Germany, France and Switzerland were closest to the silver, with less than 2 faults separating them, and Canada was the other team still in touch. But hope was very much alive for Britain because discarding Tim's score could make a big difference to the total – if John jumped a good round. Pressure was also on the other anchormen, starting with Paul Schockemöhle. Deister had had only one fence down in the first round and looked as if he would go clear in the second, but he was foiled by the last fence, putting Germany on a grand total of 39¼ . Then Swiss rider Willi Melliger got a great improvement from Van Gogh for 8 faults and a team total of 41. The last Canadian, Ian Millar, had just one fence down on the six-year-old Big Ben, the youngest horse in the competition. His team's total was 40. Only France fell by the wayside when Jappeloup put in one of his lightening stops, catapulting Pierre Durand over his head and leaving him holding an empty bridle.

As John waited for his turn he checked with Ronnie Massarella what he had to do. 'You have to get less than 7¼ faults for the silver,' was the reply. That meant he could afford just one down. If he hit two and stayed within the time there would have been a jump-off with Canada for the bronze. John fixed his mind on the silver.

He attacked the course and straightaway he could feel Ryan was really jumping. But at fence eight, the second of the criss-crossed spreads over ditches, Ryan jumped to the left – the highest side – and a pole fell. John cursed inwardly, 'changed colour a couple of times' and faced the more difficult second part of the course. It took a brave effort to watch but it was worth every agonising second as John and Ryan cleared the rest. As Ryan bucked through the finish, John swept off his hat and waved it in triumph at the rest of the team.

Britain won the silver thanks to a great improvement in the second round. Only 12¾ faults were added to the first round total of 24. It gave them 2½ faults in hand over bronze medallists West Germany. John had earned ¾ time fault in the second round, which meant that if he had knocked down another fence, the team would have missed the chance to jump-off for bronze. The line between being a hero or a failure had never been so thin.

After the riders had received their medals, rosettes with yard-long ribbons were pinned to the horses' bridles. Then the riders could let their hair down on the victory gallop round the arena. For Steven Smith the celebration almost turned sour when his silver medal flew off the ribbon round his neck. He was distraught when he came out and was told he could not have another, so he went back in to sift the dust. With the help of the arena crew he soon found it; luckily it had not been buried by dozens of hooves.

The team celebrated in a bar at one end of the grandstand which the British equestrian teams had managed to corner for themselves and their supporters. John had been cheered on by his parents-in-law, Malcolm and Elaine Barr, as well as his father and Saint Mungo's owners, Fred and Mavis Brown. Harvey Smith had taken a couple of weeks off from his busy show programme to go to LA with his wife, Irene. They travelled between their hotel and the racecourse by bicycle. Harvey did the pedalling – he was at that time banned from driving – and Irene rode on the back. David Bowen remained the life and soul of the party, despite his disappointment at not riding. He had plenty of stories to tell of chaotic living with the lads, of shirts peeled off complete with ties, bathroom floods and striking cleaning ladies.

Before the individual championship on the last day of the Games, 12 August the riders had a few days to relax. On 11 August, Ronnie Massarella named John, Michael and Tim Grubb as Britain's competitors. Fourteen other countries entered three riders each and six more had sent a single participant, so fifty-one horses tackled the first course of fourteen fences.

The story of the competition was how Michael Whitaker lost his chance of a gold medal at a short stretch of water. In the first round Michael on Overton Amanda jumped the first of only two clears. Matching him was American Joe Fargis on Touch of Class, and five competitors were on 4 faults. In the second round, over a shorter course with fences up to 5 feet 7 inches, Michael had the advantage of going last. Tension mounted as just one competitor, Conrad Homfeld on the stallion, Abdullah, managed a clear. Touch of Class again tried her heart out; her legs seemed to disappear as she glided over the fences, but she rolled a pole off the last part of the final double. A clear round from Michael would have landed the gold.

John had never felt so nervous watching his brother. When Amanda soared over the enormous third fence – 5 feet 7 inches high, 6 feet 3 inches wide – he thought Michael was on his way to the gold. But the combination was still to come – with water ditches under the second and third parts. Because there was a wall going in, Amanda did not

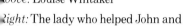

Above: Louise Whitaker

Right: The lady who helped John and
Michael polish their skills, their mother
Enid Whitaker

It's not every one-year-old that gets to wear an Olympic medal – Robert with John and
Clare

John and Ryan with silver in their sights at Santa Anita, Los Angeles

Left: 'In twenty or thirty years I will be able to look back and say "At least I have that."'

Below: HRH Prince Philip gives Ryan a pat and congratulates John after presenting the Olympic rosette

...yan shows a clean pair of heels to the fence bearing the Los Angeles Olympic emblem,
...hile 34,000 people look on

...roud moment for Donald Whitaker and his two sons

Home again, John looks to the future with one of his top horses, Saint Mungo

see the water until she was in mid-air over the first part. In that split-second her old phobia surfaced, she dropped her hind legs on the wall and started pulling up. Michael drove her over the first watery spread, which she also had down, but he had to pull her up before the next. In those moments of panic, Amanda had chalked up 11 faults and lost all hope of a medal. She hit three more fences before completing the course and had 5½ time faults, making a total of 28½ and relegating Michael to 24th of the twenty-seven riders who had qualified for the second round.

Michael said afterwards he had thought Amanda was over her water problem after clearing ditches at Aachen and Hickstead. If the first part of the combination had been poles, allowing her to see the water on the approach, he believed she would have jumped it. You could not wish for more painful proof that horses have minds of their own.

Tim Grubb finished highest of the British riders, in thir-teenth place, and would have been higher if Linky had not had the last fence in both rounds – giving him 8 of his 17¼-fault total. John was equal fourteenth on a total of 20 faults after Ryan had three down in the first round and two in the second. John said that the Olympic programme, with just two serious competitions in two weeks, had not suited Ryan. So many non-jumping days while he was super-fit had left him headstrong and lacking in concentration on the days which mattered. John wished the individual had been two days after the team event rather than four. The horse might be sixteen, but he still got too fresh when he was short of work!

The individual medal was won by Joe Fargis after a jump-off against the clock with his fellow countryman, Conrad Homfeld. Touch of Class was again foot perfect after Abdullah had had two down. In the timed jump-off for bronze, Heidi Robbiani on Jessica went first and her neat clear led to Canadian Mario Deslauriers and another Swiss, Bruno Candrian, making mistakes as they chased her time. So one of the two women and two of the three mares in the contest won medals.

* * * *

137

There was no doubt in John's mind that the Olympic silver medal was the best thing he had ever won. 'In twenty or thirty years I will be able to look back and say, "At least I have that." It overshadows everything else.' Being the top money winner did not compare with it, and even the Hickstead Derby seemed a bit of an anti-climax a couple of weeks after his return from Los Angeles. The medal also whetted John's appetite to stay amateur and have a go at getting a gold. He recognized that this decision would be partly up to the sponsors, in particular whether they wanted more publicity through having their name incorporated in the horses' names, but his inclination was against turning professional.

The 1984 season did have other highlights which were also significant pointers to the future. In the spring on the continental indoor circuit he had won his first Grand Prix on a horse other than Ryan. The breakthrough had come at Antwerp on Mr and Mrs Newton's Clonee Temple, and John got even more pleasure out of his second Grand Prix win at Dortmund, also on the chestnut mare. The course was huge and John felt he had beaten the Germans at their own game of power jumping. Dortmund was a good show for John, for he also won the championship on Clonee Temple, and one enthusiastic journalist, not knowing about her dislike of water jumps, actually tipped her as an Olympic prospect!

The second breakthrough had come in May, at Barcelona, when John rode Saint Mungo in the Nations Cup, the first time he had not had Ryan for such an event. The main difference was not knowing the horse so well: 'I did not know what Mungo would be like when there was pressure on me.' He wryly added that the pressure did not amount to much because his team mates went badly, but it was an achievement for Mungo to have the best score of the British horses. Mungo also managed a bit of one upmanship on Ryan later in the year. He went round the Hickstead Derby course – at his first attempt – with just 8 faults, delighting John, while Ryan chalked up 12 faults. 'I was not so pleased with him.'

Because John had done most of his winning at international level on Ryan there was a view, expressed by Harvey Smith in a book published in 1984, that John was a bit of a one-horse rider. Harvey said John was 'a little weak in the leg' and would only get the best out of a horse that had hold of the bridle and was really running forward. John said it was inevitable that most of his success at top level had been on one horse because Ryan had always been the best. 'If he can do the big classes better, he might as well do them and the others can be saved for another day.' Without Ryan he would have two or three horses all of about the same standard and then the pattern would change and the major challenges would be shared between them.

In fact, John's record shows a great deal of success on other horses. Indeed, it would be impossible to top the riders' league on the winnings of just one. Although Ryan had gone to far fewer shows since 1980, the old fellow never came home empty handed and at that level each rosette carried a lot of money. Even so, by 1984 Ryan was bringing in less than half the total amount won by John.

If you ask John's contemporaries what marks him as a top class rider, they will immediately say, 'He has done well on a lot of horses.' One of his friends, Geoffrey Billington, said John could adapt to all sorts of horses and gave each one tremendous confidence. As well as having recognizable skills, such as accuracy, light hands and good co-ordination, he was a thinking rider, who stayed cool whatever happened. If a horse did something strange, like dropping its hind legs in between parallel bars, many riders would be inclined to scold, which could upset the horse and make matters worse. John would just ignore the error and allow the horse to resettle. He would also always have an eye on the horse's long-term progress, rather than chasing quick wins. Geoff said he or Michael would always go like bats out of hell to try to beat the leading time, whether or not it was beatable, and this could have a bad effect on the horse. John would weigh up what his horse could do and not push it beyond that point; it might mean coming second or third that day but he would win the next.

In the best possible way John was 'calculating'. He always knew 100 per cent what he was going to do. But people often made the mistake of believing he was just as cool and sensible off the horse as he was on. He was just the opposite, witty, clever and always playing pranks. Many people have said that no one in the show jumping world has a bad word to say about John. Geoff had just one criticism: 'He's always last in the queue to buy drinks!'

As 1984 drew to a close John reached two more milestones in his career. In September, Ryan became the first British show jumper to win more than £200,000. This record came on top of Ryan's unparalleled performance in Nations Cups; from 1975 to 1984 he jumped for his country thirty-three times, completing thirty-two clear rounds.

However, the second milestone was much more significant for the future. It came in the autumn when John jumped Hopscotch in three Nations Cup competitions in North America. This earned John sufficient points to win a gold medal awarded by the international equestrian federation, the FEI. Riders gain one point for every Nations Cup in which they complete both rounds and five points for completing the team events in World and European Championships and at the Olympics. John, at 29, is only the sixth British rider to gain an FEI gold medal and the youngest by five years. The others are Sir Harry Llewellyn, Peter Robeson, David Broome, Harvey Smith and Malcolm Pyrah. Although most of John's points had come on Ryan, it boded well that both Hopscotch and Saint Mungo had contributed to the final run-up to the 50-point mark. Hopscotch had finished 1984 with a flourish, jumping a double clear for Britain at the Toronto international show. Despite going to the prize-moneyless Olympics, John had three horses in the top twenty money winners for 1984. Ryan was sixth, Clonee Temple seventh and San Salvador twentieth.

As the New Year arrived, John looked ahead to the 1985 European Championships at Dinard, France, and decided it was time he stopped relying so much on Ryan. Not that he intended to retire him just yet. The horse was still well and enjoying his jumping and John knew that his comparative inconsistency at the Olympics had been due as much to over-exuberance as to the severity of the test. However, he did feel it was no longer fair to put Ryan through a championship which involved three or four days of gruelling competition. He also realized that if the selectors had thought Ryan was past his best in 1983 they would take the same view in 1985, making it an uphill struggle for him to get in the team.

He had to look at his other rides as prospects for the major championships and he thought Hopscotch, nine in 1985, was the one to pin his hopes on for Dinard, with Saint Mungo and Rebound also contenders. 'They all have plenty of scope, they are careful and they have age on their side,' said John.

As for the horse which started it all – Ryan's Son – John believed he would never have another one as good. He planned to give him a gentle start to the season at smaller shows, see how he was and then map out his programme. After twelve years of competing together, the pressure was coming off his old friend. Ryan was already recognized as one of the best show jumpers of all time . . . and John has plenty of time to win many more medals on his successors.

APPENDIX

John Whitaker's career with Ryan's Son

1973: John starts riding Ryan's Son in June when Ryan has only 50p on his winnings card. They have instant success in novice classes, winning the Grade C Championship at Harewood Hall, Yorkshire, and Ryan reaches Grade B within three months.

1974: Ryan wins his first open competition and is Popular Open Champion at Hickstead.

John's first three-figure win comes in the Midland Bank Great Northern Championship at the Great Yorkshire Show. John caps the season with a win at the Courvoisier Championships, Wembley, and with his first trip abroad, to Zuidlaren, Holland.

1975: Victories include major classes at the Royal Show in Warwickshire and Devon County Show. He becomes Cock o' the North Champion for the first time at the Great Yorkshire.

Abroad, John jumps in his first Nations Cup for Britain at Olsztyn, Poland, where he also wins a class. Another victory comes at Dinard, France, and he jumps in the British teams at Rotterdam in Holland, and Ostend in Belgium.

1976: Year of the Montreal Olympics. John and Ryan win the Olympic trial at Cardiff and come third in the

Amateur Championship. At the Royal International Horse Show he wins more than £2,000, including second in the Grand Prix. But at Hickstead, in the final Olympic Trial, Ryan refuses and John is left out of the team for Montreal.

Ryan goes on to become Britain's top money winner of the year, winning the National Championship at Hickstead and the Calor Gas Championship at the Horse of the Year Show. He also comes equal third in the Jumping Derby.

Abroad, he jumps in Britain's Nations Cup teams at Aachen, Lucerne and Dublin.

1977: At home, his major wins come at Olympia and Devon County. John jumps for Britain at the Royal International Horse Show, Aachen, where he achieves a double clear, Washington, New York and Toronto.

1978: At home his victories include Hickstead, the Great Yorkshire (Cock o' the North), the Bass Grand National at Arena North, the Everest Double Glazing Championship at Park Farm, London. He is leading rider at the Horse of the Year Show, winning the Servis Spurs. John also wins the Masters Competition at Harwood Hall, Essex, and is leading rider at Olympia.

Abroad, he jumps a double clear in the Nations Cup in Belgium and gains his FEI bronze medal for points accumulated in international team competitions.

Ryan is the top money winning horse in Britain.

1979: John is leading rider at the Birmingham International and Olympia. Major wins come at Hickstead, Anglesey and Dortmund, West Germany.

John is in the Nations Cup teams at Geneva, Zuidlaren (double clear) and in Belgium.

1980: Year of the 'Substitute Olympics' at Rotterdam, where John wins a team silver medal and individual silver.

His major wins come at Wales and the West (Grand Prix), Aachen, Great Yorkshire, Rotterdam (in addition to the 'Substitute Olympics'), Calgary, Canada (leading rider), Dublin (Grand Prix and leading rider). He is second in the Jumping Derby at Hickstead behind younger brother Michael on Owen Gregory.

Nations Cups: Hickstead (double clear), Aachen, Calgary (double clear).

Ryan is Britain's top money winning horse for the third time and wins the Irish Horse Board's prize for the best horse bred on its soil.

1981: Year of European Championships at Munich, West Germany. John is in the British team, which comes fourth.

Ryan passes the £100,000 winnings mark. His major wins come in Holland, Munich, at the Horse of the Year Show and Bordeaux, France. Ryan wins Irish Horse Board prize again.

Nations Cups: double clears in Geneva, Dublin and Toronto. He also jumps for Britain in New York. John earns FEI silver medal for gaining more than 25 points in international team events.

Awarded British Equestrian Federation Medal of Honour.

1982: World Championships at Dublin: John is in bronze medal winning team.

He is also a bronze medallist in the World Cup final at

Gothenberg, where he wins the Grand Prix-style middle leg.

Other wins come at the Horse of the Year Show and in Brussels.

Nations Cups: Dublin (double clear), Aachen, Calgary.

1983: European Championships at Hickstead: John wins both team and individual silver medals. He also wins the Hickstead Jumping Derby with the only clear round.

Other victories come in the World Cup qualifier at Birmingham, at Gothenberg, the Royal International Horse Show (Grand Prix), Horse of the Year Show.

Nations Cups: Dublin and Calgary (double clear).

John and Michael gain £30,000 a year each in sponsorship from Next, the fashion shop chain. Both brothers are put on the Olympic short-list.

Ryan is top money winner for the fourth time.

From 1973 to 1983 John also enjoyed success on a variety of horses which backed up Ryan's Son at home and abroad. These include Singing Wind, Golden Vale, Askern, Rush-green, Charlie's Angel and Saint Mungo.

1984: With Ryan being saved for the Olympics, his other rides play an even more important role. On Clonee Temple he wins Grand Prix at Antwerp and Dortmund.

On Hopscotch, he wins the Grand Prix at Barcelona and on Saint Mungo he has a victory at Aachen.

Saint Mungo is the first horse other than Ryan which John

rides in a Nations Cup – at Barcelona and Aachen. Hopscotch jumps in Nations Cups in Washington, New York and Toronto (double clear).

With Ryan, John clinches the Olympic silver medal for the British team in Los Angeles by completing the second round with only one fence down.

He also jumps Ryan in the Nations Cup at Calgary. By September Ryan's total winnings amount to more than £200,000.

By the end of 1984 John has earned more than 50 points in Nations Cups, which entitles him to an FEI Gold Medal.*

*One point is gained for each Nations Cup in which the rider completes both rounds. Five points are awarded for completing the Olympic, World and European Championship team competitions.

146

INDEX